D0838769

In America's Court

In America's Court

How a Civil Lawyer Who Likes to Settle
Stumbled into a Criminal Trial

Thomas Geoghegan

THE NEW PRESS
NEW YORK

To R. C. and Jack

Published in the United States by The New Press, New York, 2002
Distributed by W. W. Norton & Company, Inc., New York

LIBRARY OF CONGRESS CATALOGING-IN-PUBLICATION DATA
Geoghegan, Thomas.
In America's court : how a civil lawyer who likes to settle stumbled into a
criminal trial / Thomas Geoghegan.
p.   cm.
ISBN 1-56584-732-6 (hc.)
1. Criminal courts—United States—Anecdotes.   2. Criminal justice,
Administration of—United States—Anecdotes.   3. Practice of law—
United States—Anecdotes.   4. Lawyers—United States—Anecdotes.
5. Geoghegan, Thomas.
K184 .G46 2002
345.73'01—dc21
2002020065

The New Press was established in 1990 as a not-for-profit alternative to the large,
commercial publishing houses currently dominating the book publishing industry.
The New Press operates in the public interest rather than for private gain, and
is committed to publishing, in innovative ways, works of educational, cultural,
and community value that are often deemed insufficiently profitable.

The New Press, 450 West 41st Street, 6th floor, New York, NY 10036
www.thenewpress.com

Printed in the United States of America

2   4   6   8   10   9   7   5   3   1

CONTENTS

PART TWO: "THAT'S WHY YOU GO TO LAW SCHOOL"

INTRODUCTION
"THIS IS YOUR TRIAL DATE!"

Len R. claims, "The worst thing they taught us in law school is that to be a 'real' lawyer, you have to try cases."

"Oh?" I start my "cross," as I like to do with close friends. "You don't think that's *true,* do you?"

Yet I think even some of us who are "civil litigators" must know: This idea that we have to try cases is a lot of crap. Only if I pass as a civil litigator (and I do) . . . how do I live with this? If none of my cases ever go to trial, well. . . .

Am I a real lawyer?

I just looked up, for all the federal courts, how many "civil" cases are pending right now. Number?

Over one hundred thousand.

But each year how many do in fact go to trial?

Just about three thousand.

That's bench, without a jury. Jury cases, even fewer. Now, consider that out there we have a *million* or so lawyers. Why do so few push to trial? Easy to say, "Part of it's because of fear!" How silly: *All* of it's because of fear! Take my own life. As a trial lawyer, I may go another twenty more years always on the verge of, but never "in," a trial. When I was younger, I'd be on what the older judges called their "trailing trial calendar," and that means that "my" case, slowly, like a panther, is trailing *me,* climbing up the judge's docket like a tree, and when it's at the top . . . it leaps!

Sometimes no warning, or just a few hours. The judge's clerk will phone: "Counsel? You ready, counsel? Next Monday it's your turn to go!"

And I'm on the other end, and I'm shouting, "No, no! Monday? No! This can't be. . . ." As if the clerk decides this! (She might.)

And then I wake up. Because in real life, it never happens.

But they are always giving you trial dates. The other day before a magistrate judge, I was given one. He is a magistrate, that is, a kind of assistant judge. If a Democrat, the poor wretch is now stuck as an assistant. This one is wiry, thin, austere with all of us in a Jesuitical pop-quiz way. He seemed to be looking at me especially when he said:

"Gentlemen . . . September fifteenth. Okay? *This is your trial date!*"

And he said it, "This-is-your-trial-date," as if he were our counselor, and we were entering the Twelve Steps, and he had to speak to us in a certain way, like: "See? September fifteenth. It's yours. It's your date now. You 'own' it."

We nodded.

"Don't come back later and say, 'Judge, I have another trial, or . . . I have a personal problem. My wife is . . . ' No. It's *yours.*"

We own it.

I had come in for just a short hearing on preliminary injunction, but now he had set us for a full trial, speeded up. I was going to say, "What's the rush?" But I was the one who had filed the damn thing. Looking up, he said as an afterthought, of small importance:

"I should tell you, since it is now set for September fifteenth . . . that I have four other trials starting the same day."

What? All the lawyers stared at each other: FOUR?

"But it's my experience," he said, "that all four of these will settle. So be ready. We're going ahead."

Bam, he shut the book, and then we left. So the big day, September 15, comes, and four trials plus ours are set to go. All at once. Before the same judge.

So?

What happened?

I have no idea because of course we settled. But when September 15 did come, I remembered, "This is my trial date!" And how much I wanted to go over to the court on the day the five trials were set, but I was afraid. Afraid? Yes. I was afraid to walk in . . .

And no one would be in court.

Once, I used to tutor in a boys' home, and each Tuesday night, my "student" would ask, "Oh! This week, were you . . . IN COURT?"

Yeah, kid. I was in court.

One night I could even see myself before Judge O. It had been a status hearing, of course. Not a trial. A status is when a judge may ask . . . well, anybody take a deposition lately? This was a civil rights case.

"So?" said the judge to me. "Have you made an offer to settle?"

When I stammered, it must have irked him.

"Come on," he snapped, "we *know* it's going to settle."

I blushed, furious. Okay, but does he have to say it, on the *record?* Normally, judges say, "Now, remember, I urge the parties . . . I encourage you all . . . to settle, and I will make my office available at any time . . . blah, blah, blah. . . ." But to say what he said now went too far.

"Your Honor, I . . . ," I said. "I . . . of course I made an offer to settle." (No doubt I did say something to her.)

Now I took a step left, as if to nudge my opposing counsel: Your turn. But the judge kept pressing me. "You did?"

I nodded.

"In dollars and cents?" he asked. "Did you make it in *dollars and cents?*"

"No, not yet, Judge."

He knew that it's hard for nonmath types like us to figure out the lost health, lost pension, etc. "Okay," he said. "I'm going to put it in the minute order that by . . . next status, you will make an offer in dollars and cents."

Wait, can he do that? Of course it may be true that 95 percent of all civil cases settle. Or at least that's like the "bar" fact: I don't know where the figure comes from, really. But still for Judge O. to say what he did! And to say it in front of six rows of lawyers! And in front of my opposing counsel!

Who's a woman. Which doesn't matter. But it makes it worse, as if the judge is saying, Ha! Don't have the guts, huh, to go against her?

Of course that's not what he means. It's just . . .

I'm used to this now. I go in, I listen to their sarcasm. A judge the other day, as I was going on about big plans for discovery, cut me off, right in the middle, and said, "Counsel."

"Your Honor?"

"Is this a *real* case?"

I knew what he meant. So in my real voice, I whispered, "It is, Judge."

"Yeah. Okay. I just wanted to know."

Actually it wasn't a real case, but I thought he had a nerve to ask. It's odd how they are getting bolder in the way they talk to us. In chambers the other day before Judge L., there were six or seven lawyers, and two did the talking, and the rest of us nodded. "Your Honor," one of the lead counsel was saying, "we don't need a trial, we think this can be handled by summary judgment." Without a trial: by written briefs. The premise of summary judgment is that we agree on the facts but disagree about the law. Get it? No one puts on a witness.

But the judge, who, though a Reagan appointee, is a good guy, said, "Come on, can't we just try it?"

Silence. From seven lawyers. "Oh, but Judge . . . you have so many cases," one of us said. "You must be overwhelmed!"

We all nodded. He must be.

"No, I'm not really," he said. "In fact, I'm kind of looking for a case to try."

Now I could smell a bit of panic among us. "But, Judge, this is . . . it's summary judgment!"

"Oh," he said, "come on! We can try this in a day."

"But Your Honor, summary judgment will be faster!"

"No, no," he said. "You think? First I have to write an Opinion. Then do Findings of Fact. And Conclusions of Law. This 'summary' judgment is a lot of work: Come on! Can't we just *try it?*"

It took an hour in chambers to talk him out of it.

Of course many summary-judgment motions are denied. I had a friend who clerked for a judge who had a "one-inch rule." If the briefs were thicker than an inch, he would deny summary judgment automatically. "There must be a disputed fact in there somewhere."

So how do cases settle? I don't know. I can say this, truthfully, even about my own cases. It's like gentrification in my neighborhood. It's a point my friend Tony was making the other day. "You know how you drive past a building for years? Then one day it's gone. And in a few months, you can't remember: What was it that was there? Was it a Goldblatt's or . . . ? " Just as a whole Goldblatt's can disappear, so it is with some cases I work on for years. One day they're gone. And in a few months I pass a file drawer. What was it that used to be in there?

From a lawyer I saw on the El the other night I heard a good reason why our cases settle. It was late. He had a big Mr. Chips briefcase. Bulging with deps, transcripts.

"I was about to go to trial today."

"What happened?" I asked.

"Oh, she put it off. Judge ———. Last minute, she had to do some criminal case. 'Oh, you know, gentlemen, criminal comes first!' "

"Maybe," I said, "it'll settle now."

He shrugged.

"Why do you think all our cases settle?" I asked.

He thought a bit, and said, "It's not having a certain trial date."

That's right, I thought. It's the never knowing, and learning the file, learning the file, learning the file, and then . . . the day of the trial, the hangman in the hood comes out, all chirpy:

Oops! Sorry, counsel. Have to put this off.

I looked down at the guy's briefcase. "Taking the file home tonight?"

"Yeah. Might go next week." He'd get home at ten o'clock, and one of the kids would be asleep. So, alone, he'd make himself some dinner. And then I could imagine him sitting down and . . . as he chews, opening a dep. Then a vision of him eating the crinkly paper of the transcript.

Ugh. I got ill. Why are we doing this? And then it's not knowing the exact hour of our trial, that's why we give up and settle. No more! But the Next One, of course: That's the one I will try.

There are over 975,000 lawyers in the United States, or there were in 1995, which was the last attempt to count them. I phoned the American Bar Foundation to ask. "Welcome to the world of legal statistics," said an officer. "Where everything you'd think someone was counting isn't being counted." Things like:

In civil cases, who wins, who loses at trial? No one knows.

In criminal, how often is anyone out-and-out acquitted? A lot, say some. Hardly ever, say others. In other words, no one knows.

Are we overlawyered? "We have seventy percent of the lawyers in the world," says Dan Quayle.

No, says a study (which defines *lawyer* as anyone with any legal background able to appear in court). The U.S. ranks thirty-fifth in the world in "lawyers per capita."

Bolivia is ahead of us. And what country is at the very top, number one?

Vatican City, of course. Think of that, the next time you see the Pope addressing a crowd in Saint Peter's Square.

But if we don't have good numbers about many things we'd like to know, I'd like to calculate a pseudonumber of a kind: Let's start out assuming a million or so lawyers are walking around. Yet if only a few thousand cases go to trial, and if many lawyers are doing three or four trials a year, then think of all the lawyers who just stand and gape! Once, in my thirties, I did about four little trials a year. "That's a gentlemanly number," said a real trial lawyer, Tom S., at the time, when I bragged about it to him. He did even more, like eight or nine. Anyway, if all these numbers are about right, then I calculate the percentage of civil lawyers who try cases may be 2 or 3 percent. Maybe it's under *one*.

So what do the others do?

They settle. Sometimes I think the legal system is going backward. Now, we are shocked to read that, a hundred years ago, even a Clarence Darrow would bribe a jury. Whoever paid the jury the most money is who won the case. How far we've come—yes? But if Darrow were alive today, the big issue in his civil cases would be, Who is going to pay Darrow's fee? At least in Darrow's day, the opposing side did not negotiate how much to pay Darrow!

Now, in order to settle, one big part of it is whether the Opposing Side, openly, will pay us off not to try the case. In a way, it's when the Opposing Side is suddenly so nice to me that it's the creepiest to be a lawyer.

For example, the other day, in a case we are near to settling, I asked opposing counsel for an extension of time to file a brief. He said, "You want an extension?"

"I've been . . . sick, and . . ."

Like a seraph, he raised a hand. "No, no! I don't even need to hear. Your word, counsel, is good enough for me."

I mention this because three months ago the same guy was shrieking at me after court, in the hallway: "What is it with you? All you do is lie!!"

But now we're talking settlement. I remember how he started off on the phone: "Now, the first thing I want to say is, I'm sure your legal fees won't be a problem."

"Uh," I said, "don't you want to hear what they are?"

He paused. "I'm *sure* it won't be an issue."

But as I say, nobody at the American Bar Foundation is counting the number of settlements that start out this way.

Or the total dollar value of money paid every year from one lawyer to another to end a case. Yet about Darrow, who never did this, we modern types cluck: "Oh, he was corrupt. . . ."

Long ago, without my knowing it at first, it seems my classmates began dropping out. Why? Maybe they found they'd never try a case. Of late I wonder how many "lawyers," so-called, are practicing any kind of law.

A few years back, I got a call from a man who said he was in my class at law school, though I could not remember him. "I don't do much legal practice now, and I've got a case, and I thought it'd be nice to give it to someone who was in our class."

I paused. "I . . . feel awkward saying this to you, but . . . why me? We didn't really know each other."

"You're right, we didn't," he said. "And you weren't my first choice. But I've been going through our class directory . . ." (Harvard, '75) ". . . and you're the first one I've found who's still practicing law!"

What did he say next? Since I was so sick to hear this, the next minute or so is a blank. I remember putting down the phone and walking out of the office and going around the block. Oh . . . shit! I knew it. Outside as I walked . . . damn, damn, *damn!* Oh, damn it! Damn it! *Damn it!* Could I be the only—?

Just now, a memory came back to me from law school: After class one day a kid came up to me and said, "I'm really sweating this exam coming up. Of course, *you* don't have to worry."

"Me? What do you mean?"

He looked surprised. "Well, *you* aren't going to practice law, are you?" And the funny thing is, that's what I did think. And now I was the only one still doing it! And I remembered what Candy said at the party in law school. That night at the party, everyone was saying, "A lawyer should not marry another lawyer." (Bob) "No, that's right." (Molly) "I agree."

And I had said, "Gee, I'd marry a woman who was a lawyer."

And everyone started laughing, and Candy patted me, and said, "For you, it's all right. You'd be the nonlawyer in *that* relationship."

And now? Damn, I . . . oh shit, I'm the only one still doing it!

Now, that phone call was like a visitation, because I went through my class directory. There seem to be plenty of lawyers "still doing it." If you phone them up, maybe they'd admit they're just pretending. Often we are vice presidents and trustees and we are just pretending. We think we are overlawyered, but I wonder how many lawyers in the old sense there really are.

I don't want to give up being a lawyer. Now that I'm over fifty, what else could I do? But more and more I wish I could practice for a while under a whole new legal system.

France, maybe.

Yes, I wish my name could suddenly appear in a legal directory in France. Or far away. A friend of mine said the other day he wanted to work as a lawyer for the Defense Department. Why? "Oh, just to do something totally different." I, too, keep thinking that somewhere for me there is another life I have as a lawyer and I'm not being allowed to live it.

Maybe that's how I ended up at Twenty-sixth and Cal.

Part One

Twenty-sixth and Cal

1. LES ENFANTS DES . . .
TWENTY-SIXTH AND CAL

It is odd to think that I did not even notice till late in Clinton's second term that America was turning into a little bit of a gulag. We have 3,682 people on death row. Some are innocent. Some are *kids,* or legal minors at least. The prison population is close to *2 million,* or 468 prisoners for every 100,000 Americans. Twelve percent of black men between the ages of twenty and forty are in jail or prison in any given year. And while all this was happening, I'd never even gone to visit anyone in a jail. Nor in a prison. I had never dreamed of trying a criminal case.

I was too busy settling civil ones, so how could I think of doing a criminal *trial?*

It's odd, of course, that in theory I can go off and "do" one at any time. Sure, just as in theory the patriarch Abraham, in his nineties, might . . . oh, conceive a child. But in reality, I know there is such a gulf, a fiery region, between civil and criminal law, that it's hard to see how I can cross it and go over to that other shore. Besides, it's because I hate violence, murder, etc., that I thought I'd be forever on the civil side. Until recently I didn't even know that most new admissions to state prison every year are for nonviolent property, drug, or other crimes. Or that drug offenders make up most of our federal prisoners.

I am taking some of these numbers from Human Rights Watch, and its Report on the United States for 2001. As one who does mostly labor law, I turn first, of course, to the "civil" part, to read about the massive U.S. violations of labor rights. It's eerie that workers in America are spied on, fired, or run off when they try to organize, often the same as they are in Guatemala or Honduras. But now as I go on and flip through "criminal" sections, on prisons, on police torture, I wonder, in a nonhysterical way, if there is such a big gulf between civil and criminal. Perhaps *all* of it is simply human rights law. Conditions in our prisons often violate clauses of the U.N. Convention on Torture, and this may be related to the way, more and more, each decade, we trample on labor rights, or the fact that the National Labor Relations Board, just in this past year, adjudicated over 24,000 illegal firings. So maybe there is a connection, the thinnest of threads, that ties even me to criminal law. Maybe there is no civil, no criminal law, but only the law of nations, and that's the law I should be doing.

For my first twenty years after law school, I think the only criminal court I ever stepped into was in Paris. It was the Palais de Justice, which I saw, by accident, in 1977, when I was on vacation. I had met a grad student named Didi, who took me around, and everywhere we went he'd say:

"This used to be a red-light district."

And:

"This used to be a red-light district."

And:

"This used to be a red-light district."

And he pointed out the battle scenes from the great student revolt, in May 1968:

"This is where we fought the cops."

And:

"This is where we fought the cops."

By a wild mistake, I had ended up crashing in his student flat, but Didi was a perfect host. I'd wake up every morning, and eat nothing, but I'd drink the blackest of black coffee, from a cup as big as the bell in Notre Dame. And while I was sipping, Didi, already up, would be poring over his favorite paper, *Libération,* and one morning he threw down the paper and said, if I can quote this right, "We must go to Expedites." Or it was like Les Expedites, or some special court that he had just read about in a Maoist paper. On the way over, Didi told me of this court, which was a new court, and how judges could deport Tunisian kids who'd been picked up the night before. Now, being a lawyer on vacation, I was aghast that we were going into a criminal court. (Because I did this all the time? In fact I'd never done it. But I didn't want to start in Paris.)

But Didi insisted. The Palais has an icy, Bourbon front, with a warning over the door: *Liberté, Egalité, Fraternité.* So when we came in, I was shocked to see a crowd. The place was full of people, like Didi, like me, really, who, if they had been Americans, would never have been here. "Who are all these people?" I asked, but Didi was intent, staring, so I looked in that direction: There was a Tunisian or Moroccan boy standing in a golden light. The gold of the light in which the boy was standing seemed to have caromed off the Louvre and fallen on his olive skin.

And in my very goose bumps at this moment, I must have experienced what a philosopher might call the sensuous apprehension of the idea of Justice!

Or wait, wasn't it the idea of Injustice? After all, the boy was going to be deported! But what I see now in my mind is not just this boy but the boy in this golden light being stared at by Didi, and me, and Didi's girlfriend, and twenty or thirty people who were buzzing on the French coffee they'd sipped that morning as they read it all, with horror, in *Libération.* That golden light: Wasn't it the light I had seen the day before in the Bibliothèque Mazarine, where Didi had sneaked us in? It was like the light of the Louvre, the light of the French Enlightenment, and the light of the Declaration of the Rights of Man, and the way it was streaming all over this boy, I knew it was like a vision. All I could think was:

Behold this boy, in the light of the Louvre.

Then I also began to behold his lawyers: two young men, as young as me, pacing in their black gowns, arguing and waving their arms, and they were both emotional and logical in a certain French way, or a way Descartes might have written about if he'd been describing the French: I think, therefore . . . I am irate! The way the two waved their arms, that was part of the vision too. Although I didn't understand a word, I knew that they were arguing not only for the boy but also for the Rights of Man, and that for them, Africa was not just a gravel pit for digging up a diamond to give to your mistress, it was a place from which one could come and be treated with the respect of a citizen of France. After we left, Didi gripped my hand, I think, or we had some moment of fraternité, because I was a lawyer, too, and I would be going back to Chicago and waving my arms and surely I'd be arguing for these same things as well. And at this moment I did think I would go back and argue for the Rights of Man, but when I got back home, I went right back to doing civil. And while I tried a few cases, mostly I settled.

Twenty-one years went by.

Of course I had more or less forgotten about Paris. Then one day in our building I ran into Scott.

Now, for years I had been saying to Scott, who does criminal, "We should do a case together." But I said that in the way you say, One day we should have lunch together. It was sometime in February when he came up and said, "Look, if you ever want to do this, I have a case that's coming up. This . . . this would be a good one."

What?

I was so rattled that as he began to describe this case, I couldn't catch a word. "Well," I said, upset, "when . . . I mean, when would we do this?"

I already knew, no way, it's impossible, I have way too much work.

"Next Monday."

"Next Monday?" I was about to say why I couldn't possibly do it. And then I had a creepy, sick feeling that maybe, after all . . . OH

SHIT, WHAT IF I COULD DO THIS? I . . . but no, it wasn't possible, I had work, I had . . . but what if I really didn't have work and I could do this?

"Well, how long would it take?"

"Oh, it'll go fast, maybe three days."

"I don't . . . no, I . . . I don't think I can." And now I remembered, when a few months back Scott had asked me before, I had begged off: "Scott, I . . . all I could do would be second chair. I couldn't do anything as a principal, I couldn't really, like, try the case."

"No." He smiled. "That'd be malpractice."

Now, this annoyed me, in part because it would be malpractice. But hadn't I been in the Louvre? Okay, yet like every small-firm lawyer I think, It must be something like a divorce, or a will, or an SEC filing. If I *had* to, I could learn it as I go along. Practice on the client.

But it would be malpractice. I do try cases, right? I'm supposed to be a litigator, though I can't remember when one of my cases last went to trial. So why couldn't I do criminal? But as a civil lawyer told me once, "Yes, I could try the facts, but I don't know the *system,* what is let in, what is kept out." More important, as another civil lawyer friend said, "Who do you cut the deals with?"

I guess Scott would know. My question was, Where *is* this "criminal" court? Okay, it's at "Twenty-sixth and Cal" ("Cal" is for California Avenue), way south of the Loop. How do you get there?

No, I had work. Only, things had cleared up. Wasn't I working only part of this Saturday?

"I can't."

Scott seemed not to hear. "Can we meet this weekend?"

"I can't." Client . . . I had to meet him this Saturday.

"Can I give you the file?"

(What? And on Monday just show up?) "I . . . Scott, I won't have time to look at it."

Then he said, "Well, just remember this: We're meeting at nine o'clock, and it's in the courtroom of Judge K."

"Judge K., okay" I nodded. As if I was going. . . .

I didn't mean okay, I was going . . . just, I'd think about it. Only, now he was expecting me!

Shit, I can't do it, it's a waste of three days. It's not that I think They're All Guilty, but . . . anyway, where *is* this Twenty-sixth and Cal?

Why, some may ask, would he need me, a "second chair"? Funny, I'd not have asked that. I knew Scott often did a jury case by himself. But it's like trying to sail, by yourself, a three-deck, twenty-gun man-of-war. You can be a hell of a sailor, but you go nuts, all by yourself, running up and down, swabbing the deck, getting the damn mainsail to stop flapping. At least I could help mark the exhibits. Do you know what it's like to have someone next to you hand you the exhibit so that you can give every part of your brain to the framing of the next question? So why can't a paralegal do this?

Answer: A paralegal could. But who can afford one?

Yet if it were me, I'd want a lawyer, too, because there's just something about a lawyer . . . the woolen suits, I don't know. While you're up there before the judge, your fellow lawyer can whisper:

"Scott, look out . . . behind you! The prosecutor, he's got a knife!"

Or:

"Your collar's up!"

I don't know why, but I'd trust a lawyer before I would a paralegal, since a lawyer knows what it's like to get a knife in the back.

Friday afternoon, Scott dropped off the file while I was out. I thought, I should phone him, and tell him I can't go. But I got busy and I forgot. It was Friday, and for once I had been in court, on an oral argument, before a state judge, who had said, "Counsel, I've read your papers. Now, is there anything *not* in those papers you have to add?"

"Yes, Your Honor." (There must be, right?) So I talked for ten minutes.

The judge stared at me awhile when I was done. "Counsel," he said, "you have added NOTHING."

And he ruled against me.

On the way back, Amy, my co-counsel, said, "He likes you, though."

"He doesn't 'like' me."

It was a stupid motion, and a stupid case . . . and why was I doing this for a living? I went back to the office and filled out a time sheet:

"Appear in court . . . and ADD NOTHING . . . 1.5 hours."

I was sick of it, and it was Friday, and I had to meet a client, no, just a "potential" client, on Saturday. And even if it were just an hour, it befouled the whole day.

And Monday when I woke up, I remembered that Scott was still expecting me at nine A.M., at some place I'd never been. Oh, God, why didn't I call him? The only thing to do was just go down, somehow, and say, "Scott, I'm sorry, I can't do it," and go back up to the Loop. How did I get into this? Should I drive? No. I'd get lost.

No, better to take the El into the Loop, then I'd splurge on a cab and let the cab driver find it. So I took the Ravenswood, the little yuppie choo-choo train that is for everyone who is white and under thirty and goes choo-choo around the Loop, and then I got in a cab and said, "Twenty-sixth and Cal."

Well, I'd have never figured out the way, since to my surprise, he drove west, on I-290, the Eisenhower. Then he got off and drove about twenty blocks to the south. To think, a downtown lawyer would drive this—every day!

Maybe I should look at the file.

Now I remembered, Scott had said, "This'll be a good one." The client was fifteen. Years old, fifteen? No. He'd been in jail for seven years.

Maybe it said that here. No, it didn't say.

It was something about a felony murder. A holdup. He had been arrested . . . or no, he was convicted, at fifteen. Holdup in a bar. Bunch of kids. But he was twenty-two now? He was having a new trial or . . .

I couldn't figure it out, so I looked out the window. "Oh, the city's coming back!" friends of mine say. Even over by the Henry Horner Homes, as if Henry Horner is the Western Edge of the World, and it's like they think the World ends at Western Avenue. They should take a trip out here.

Like I am doing, every day.

The cabbie in the front seemed to know what I was thinking: "It's a disgrace, isn't it?" He looked out at the boarded-up houses. "It's a disgrace a great city would let this stuff stay up, isn't it?"

What, did he drive carriages on Michigan Avenue? Something about this guy made me think, I'm being hit up for a tip.

It was March, rainy. We passed a bar, boarded up. "I bet," I said, "they're closed because it's Saint Patrick's Day."

I was curious what he'd say. But he was wary, and clammed up.

I got out at the court, which had the look of a normal Public High School. That is, it looked dangerous. In fact, there were five or six kids, gang types, hanging out in front. But this couldn't be a Public School: I didn't see any cops.

Even when I walked inside, I saw only a cop or two, who waved me through. Not just me. Everyone. The detector must have been busted, since I usually set it off. This worried me.

Of course I worry in Federal, where they frisk you and it takes five minutes. I have to raise my arms, take off my belt . . . yes! . . .

while on the other side of the plate glass, I can see a Ryder van, in a tow zone, as it softly ticks away.

But I like that better than being waved through. Even though I was in a hurry, I was so upset by this that I went over to a guard, to show my lawyer's ID.

WOULD YOU PLEASE LOOK AT IT!

Okay, okay, he looked. If that's what I wanted.

What a place. Where was Judge K.? And I was jumpy, because it hit me, when I stepped out of the cab, how will I get back? No cabs came down here.

Shit . . . but anyway, I had to find Scott. "Judge K.?" I asked.

"Sixth floor," someone said.

"Uh . . . how do I get a cab if I want to get to the Loop?"

"Cabs? Here?" But I was running to find Scott. What a "Court"! Until then I had only been in courts designed by Mies van der Rohe, or a Mies wannabe, so to me every court had to be simple:

Black

White

And chilling. Really, it has to remind me of the stage set for *The Duchess of Malfi.* I mean a particular production of it I saw years ago; it's a blood tragedy. Revenge. And when the curtain rose, I had to gasp at the set, the black and white of the tiles, the pillars, even the dresses of the women, it was all in black and white, and everyone, in black and white, was proceeding, slowly, step by step, in single file, across the stage:

Step

by step,

by step.

Somehow it all reminded me of federal court. The same cold Miesian-type beauty. A beauty that at any moment might drown us in a world of blood.

But Twenty-sixth and Cal? It's like a bus stop. Sure, they wave you through. Who would bother to blow up a Trailways?

Come on, elevator. It was nine o'clock, I ran and . . . ah, I found Judge K. There was Scott, who let out a breath. "Hi," he said. "I was preparing an order . . . you know, for 'leave' for you to appear."

Now I felt bad. It came to me again what a decent guy this is. Everyone respected Scott. He had been editor of his law review. Went to a fancy Loop firm. But he wanted to be a public defender. So he took the bonus he got from the firm, and he and his wife blew the whole thing at a commune in Scotland. Like a Lindisfarne. Sad, these kids who missed the sixties. "But Scott," I once said, "even in the sixties, I didn't know anyone who went to Lindisfarne!" And the tough city-lawyer side of him can laugh at that, but the fact is: He *went* there.

But back to what makes him amazing: He really is a decent guy.

So how could I go back? Besides, no cabs. So, okay, I'll stay a bit.

Scott took the order for my "leave to appear" up to Judge K. Odd. He was just sitting there, by himself. No lawyer, no case in front of him. Was he waiting for a cab, too? He saw my name, and said it not as *Ga-gen,* but *Ga-ha-gen.* He joked, "I'm giving it the South Side pronunciation," which was an erudite thing to say. Because it *was* the South Side pronunciation, and he let me know that he must know the other, Lace Curtain pronunciation, which my family uses because, of course, we're descended from lawyers. I smiled. Though I'm not true "Irish," hey, let him think so. He might not be Greek. The Greeks are very proud of their judges, though. My first Loop parade, it was for Greek Americans, and on the podium there was a man with a mike shouting, "And today . . . today . . . we honor, honor . . . ALL the great men of Greek heritage, and we honor . . . PLATO, and . . . SOCRATES, and . . . SOPHOCLES, and . . .

A slight breath: ". . . JUDGE STAMOS!"

And he would have said Judge K., too, but I don't think he was a judge then. Anyway, I liked the way Judge K. made the joke. As it turned out, he'd often use his wit as a way to deflect his own temper, and when something dark began building up, he seemed to catch it and make it go pop, and turn it into a joke. Only sometimes if the joke did not come fast enough, he'd go KA-BOOM! Anyway, he signed the order.

Scott said, "Let's go back and see Rolando."

Who? I had no idea. I inferred it was our client. So I followed Scott to a side door, which he opened.

On the left was the Judge's "Chambers," big enough to stick a broom in, and then I looked stupidly to my right and saw . . .

I saw . . .

I . . .

Well, I saw . . . a cage, iron bars, something that as a lawyer I had never seen before, except on TV. And I was irked, because I knew I should have expected this.

I had thought I was going to be in a cab by now. Somebody, Scott I guess, was saying, ". . . holding cell . . . ," or ". . . lockup . . . ," and ". . . this is the lockup."

So I guess what I saw must have been—well, the "lockup." But it was SIX FEET from the Judge's chamber! Before I could gasp, I . . .

I, uh, saw . . .

. . . this . . . kid. Our client. Standing in a golden light, and all I could think was—

He's innocent! That's all, like a sunburst. Then it was as if it all went dark, and then . . . when a weak light came up, I saw him again, and Scott said his name:

"Rolando."

I looked at Scott: You have to get him *out*. Skip I-was-in-Prison, you-visited-Me; Get him in a cab or something. By the way, this light was not "golden" but yellow. Really, the color of urine. Light like piss running down the walls. Where did it come from? I couldn't see a light bulb.

Then I saw pitchforks on the wall. Little black marks on a dirty yellow. Drawings of Satanic things . . . which made that Stone Age cave at Lascaux seem like the Bibliothèque Mazarine.

How did drawings of gang symbols get here, a few feet from where the judge was sitting? "Rolando," Scott was saying.

The kid, six foot two, was bending over to listen. As if in the dark, in a mushroom way, he'd grown up tall enough, in prison here, but sort of crooked.

It's funny, or sick, but I had a desire for Rolando to talk to me. (Me too!) But what could I say?

Say, Rolando, I'm a labor lawyer from the Loop . . . and hey, you shouldn't be in here. Do you know that?

Or: Hello, I'm second chair?

Somehow, I now knew: Rolando was in here for "felony murder." That means, he didn't kill anyone, but he's guilty of murder anyway. It seems that two older kids, seventeen or eighteen, ran into him and pulled him along as they held up a bar. Said: "You be the lookout." The kid who was seventeen shot a customer. So under "felony murder," anyone who is mixed up in a holdup . . .

. . . unarmed, no gun, fifteen, walking along . . .

is guilty of murder too. So he was convicted, and since fifteen he'd been in here, might be in for forty more. But by a freak, he was going to get a second trial.

And why had this taken so long? I don't know. All I knew was, number one, We Had to Get Him Out. And number two, well . . . In the courtroom behind Judge K., there was a big oil portrait of John Marshall, first chief justice of the United States Supreme Court, and for the whole morning I looked at it and thought, What's a picture of a federal judge doing in state court? (Was it a used one, from Goodwill?)

And: Does the chief justice know that on the other side of the wall, there are pitchforks behind his *head?*

Judge—don't look!

And as I wondered at this, Scott was saying something very strange to Rolando, but I want to pause in the story.

2. A PAUSE IN THE STORY

Stopping the story, which is a bad thing, I have to explain why I knew this kid was innocent. I'll cut the crap about the light. Perhaps instead it was a "meme." In the science of evolution, the meme is a trait, or practice, even a moral practice, which we are said to pass along in our genes. If I understand this, it's like a twitch or a shudder.

So outside the cell, I may have shuddered, because I "knew" that as a species we just don't put our young away like this, in prisons with adults.

Still, I could be wrong to say this is a meme. But long before Darwin, people like Kant wrote that our species was evolving, in secret, toward a—a what? Toward a "perfect civil constitution." It was our history, as a species. That we would end up with certain laws. Treaties. These would codify the twitches, the habits, that we were starting to pass along, as if in our genes.

Indeed, at that moment, though I didn't know it, there really was a Kant-like treaty that codified what I felt. This is the U.N. International Convention on the Rights of the Child. Ever hear of it? No. But it urges every country not to lock up a kid like Rolando with adults. It also says not to execute them either. And because there is a meme behind it, every country has ratified the Convention on the Child, except of course Iraq and—

Us. The U.S.

So it seems in America not everyone has the meme. Or maybe in our "island," we are evolving a different type of mammal, just as Darwin found on the Galápagos Islands. What scares me about our island is that the people without the memes are propagating faster, or at least faster than me.

Look at Justice Scalia, on the Supreme Court, who clearly does not have this meme. In one of his opinions, he scoffed at the claim that the norms of the Bill of Rights might reflect the norms of international law. No, just because it may be part of the human standard of decency, that doesn't mean it's part of the *American* standard of decency.

The justice also has many, many more children than I do. So, like on Galápagos, we may be evolving in a different way, or anyway, there just may be no such thing as memes.

Besides, at the moment I flinched, I knew nothing of this Convention on the Child. I felt a shudder, and later I thought it might just be a ghastly presentiment that I was standing . . . right then . . . in a pool of human blood. Of course at the time there was no blood, but I read in the paper a few months later that a prisoner was beaten to death—in a place like the place where, at this moment, as a civil lawyer I was standing.

And even if I can't believe in memes, I do of course believe in ghosts.

3. NEW CLOTHES

Strange as it sounds, Scott was talking to Rolando about clothes. "I thought your mom'd be here," he was saying.

Rolando spoke, but I couldn't hear.

"Well," said Scott, "we'll have to go down and meet her. Then I'll bring your clothes up and you can change. . . . Then we can pick the jury." After more talk, we left and went down to meet his mom, who was bringing a new, store-bought suit for Rolando. "I didn't want the jury to see him in prison clothes," Scott said.

I gulped. "Scott, has he been in there for seven years?"

"Yeah."

Okay, I'd not read the file, but come on! He was innocent. And even when I knew nothing, I know when something is ridiculous. SEVEN YEARS?

By the way, Scott never said Rolando was "innocent." He would say what a decent kid he was, hardworking, etc. "Did I tell you, he has a fiancée?"

"What? This kid?"

If he went in at fifteen, how could he have a fiancée? By now we were downstairs at the detector, and waiting for his mom.

I was amazed: Case about to start, and we're waiting for the laundry. "What's his mom look like?"

"She's real short. Maybe I should phone."

Come on, hurry up, lady! And down here, as the shock of being in the cell wore off, I began to "hear" what Scott had had to tell Rolando. "Look," Scott had been saying to the boy, "I have to ask you this, okay?"

Rolando had frozen.

"I have to give you the State's offer." It was a plea agreement to let the boy serve just twenty-eight more years. Twenty-eight. Years.

And the boy had made a soundless NO! and it was awful to hear such a soundless thing, like from nowhere on this earth. May I never hear that sound of NO again. Though more awful, I think, if instead he had said YES.

. . . yes.

Waiting for his mom, I was now staring at the courthouse grill. What Scott said they called the Gangbangers Lounge. With little iron bars on which they grilled the hot dogs. As I watched those little rolling iron bars and heard the popping of the grease, I felt ill. I had to get out . . . to *anywhere,* anyplace where people drank Tropicana Orange Juice, Not from Concentrate. If only I could be at a status hearing in federal court!

If I stayed down here, what could I even drink? *Coke?*

Thank God at this moment I saw his mom, sort of. For it's true, she was really short. Though the suit was brand-new, she'd decided she had to clean it. Okay. We ran upstairs. Here, Rolando. Come on! Trial was starting, five minutes, etc. Rolando went off, with a woman deputy, then he came out, and . . .

UGH.

It was a Nehru jacket! God, he looked like he was a lieutenant in the Confederate Army. Also, the sleeves were too long.

"It's nice," said the deputy. I gathered Rolando's fiancée had picked it out.

"It's nice," said Scott, frowning, "but we have to get this tag off."

"Tag?" I couldn't see it. Scott held up Rolando's arm, and on the sleeve it said STREET SMART. Oh. Can't let the jury see that. We now had no time, but Scott was frantic, pulling out the threads. "We need a scissors," he said.

Trial is about to start!

Then the deputy said, softly, "I'll get a scissors," and I admired her for sneaking any sharp object in here, but it turned out she just had a pair of tweezers. But as word spread she had a scissors, a whole mob of people, deputies, clerks, began crowding like penguins to watch.

The deputy—cut! Off! And Scott could smile at last.

I turned, gasping. Penguin people! Clear the way!

4. "WHAT'S YOUR FAVORITE RADIO STATION?"

Judge K. started with a roar. Today? We'd pick a jury. Then both sides would do openings. Then . . . oh, we'll do a witness or two. Many a judge talks like this, but Judge K. really did go fast. But then the State's Attorney—a woman, I noticed—said what She, the State, was going to do. Today, she said, we'd just pick a jury, and "we won't have our witnesses until tomorrow."

Judge K. was very quiet. Well, who wears the pants here? With a judge and a state's attorney, it can seem, to an outsider, like an old married couple. Sometimes a state's attorney will almost seem to run things.

Sometimes, a state's attorney will be very quiet.

I just hoped they wouldn't argue. Of course, I myself blow up a lot. In law, I find that as I get older and more experienced . . . the more I lose my temper. And yet, I *hate* the fighting.

So I was amazed when Scott, who is so nice, said, "I like the adversary system."

You do?

But I must say, the State's Attorney, Ms. M., was okay. By the way, she had a lovely name, but I'd rather not give it here, since at trial I came to like her.

And when I say "I liked her," I mean what another lawyer friend, L., who once tangled with her said: "Well, I don't dislike her."

Even when she was tough with Rolando, I never *disliked* her, so in that sense, I actually liked her.

And her co-counsel was Mr. S., who tried part of the case since he was a true "second chair," and not like me, who just sat in a chair. In fact at first I didn't even think that these people around me might be here for the jury. Every case I try . . . *when* I used to try them . . . is a bench trial. No jury. I only see the judge. So while I truly am a "trial lawyer," I could truthfully turn to Scott and say, "Who are those people?"

At first I thought they were court watchers. But they were pretty young for that, so I didn't get it.

Scott said that was the jury. At the moment he spoke, though, it was as if an angel in a dream were saying to me, also, *That* is the jury.

Or at least it was the jury pool. After all my years of hopelessly inputting "JURY DEMANDED" on so many of my complaints, since it is malpractice not to do so . . . it was a shock for me finally to see one, in my old age, and realize that now: Yes, we're going to pick a jury!

Out came the first "panel." Scott pushed a pad over as the first candidate was up: "Think of some questions to ask." But what? The only one that matters, "What are your politics?," you aren't allowed to ask. Well . . . *Do you believe there is such a thing as the sensuous apprehension of the idea of Justice?*

Yes or no!

Instead I wrote down on the pad, *What's your favorite radio station?* In jury selection, it's true, *everyone* asks that.

Now, in New York, the lawyers themselves can ask questions of the jurors. I hear that they can get personal. "Have you ever been raped? What was that like for you?"

In New York people expect hardball. In Chicago, though, a judge has to clear the questions. And Judge K., on *his* voir dire, liked to be discreet. For example, as if to save you from embarrassment, he wouldn't ask, "Are you married or are you single?" He'd glance at a note and then *tell* you:

"You're a married person."

Or: "You're a single person."

As a juror, you just had to nod. But once during voir dire, to my surprise, he asked a woman (yuppie), from Lincoln Park, "Do you live with anyone?"

"Y-yes . . . my cat," she said, her voice breaking.

Same thing he asked of a night-school student. "My . . . my mother," said the poor guy.

Heh, heh. But what would I have said? "Uh . . . J-judge, I just go home at night and read."

When David Souter was nominated for the Supreme Court, a woman who tends to mother me called me up: "From what I read of this Souter, he's a bachelor, he lives alone, all he does is go home at night and read. My question is, Why don't they nominate *you?*"

Maybe if the structure of our government seems to be collapsing, or imploding (with filibusters, impeachment, Special Prosecutors), it's only because we have now kicked away the very foundation of our state, the cornerstone . . . which is the jury. Edmund Burke once claimed that the whole machinery of the British state existed, in the end, just to swear in "twelve men, good and true," as members of an ordinary British jury.

If I haven't seen a jury until this very morning, the simple reason is that juries aren't a foundation of anything now. This arises from the fact that we have moved away from a system of common law based on precedent, on community memory. We now have a system where judges decide everything. Really, we have a European-type "civil law" system, though we won't admit it in our law schools. And while the right wing complains of judicial activism, it's absurd, because many on the Right are pushing this civil-law-type system. Justice Scalia is a good example. To a real conservative, the traditional common law is the worst kind of law, because judges can make up things, and say, "Well, that's *always* been our history," etc. There's no check on this kind of legal fantasy. Anyway, it's hard to have a system based on memory, tradition, etc., when Congress is passing a hundred new laws every year, to keep up with Microsoft, G.E., etc. Remember, this common-law, jury stuff was invented for the Middle Ages! When nothing happens. So if it's fine for 1100 A.D. under King John, it's not in a country where, every year, even Count Chocula cereal undergoes some "revolutionary" change. In civil law it's almost malpractice to cite a "precedent" that's older than three years. As for juries, many upright people can't remember who, if anyone, came before Britney Spears.

If we still let ordinary people fiddle with cases at Twenty-sixth and Cal, it may be that nothing much here is at stake. "Real" lawyers don't come down here, do they?

So, though I'm a trial lawyer, that's why I just don't know how to pick a jury.

When I first did a nonjury trial long ago, I found a trial handbook, published in the 1920s. There was a chapter (and it was serious) on "How to Pick Juries." It was easy. For a plaintiff, it's best to pick:

Irish

Jews

and . . . be careful . . . some of the countries in southern Europe. For a defendant, it's best to head north, to find:

Germans, and especially—

Norwegians.

In fact, this book I had went nuts over Norwegians.

When I showed this to my colleague Len, he laughed. "Pretty old-fashioned."

And it *is* old-fashioned, since the whole thing's unusable if people intermarry. As late as the 1970s, on the radio one night I heard a group of old lawyers complain, "Can't pick a jury anymore! You put on some gal named O'Hara? Irish? Turns out she's half German."

(Like me.)

Or even worse, Ms. O'Hara is *all* German, and she just married an "O'Hara." This may be another reason we don't use juries anymore.

•   •   •

So all you can ask is, What's your favorite radio station?

Scott said, "I'd like to ask about coercion." It was our defense, of course, that Rolando was coerced. That two older kids (seventeen, eighteen) had forced him (fifteen) to be part of the holdup, as their lookout. In Rolando's first trial, the judge did not let the jury consider this as a defense, or at least there was no instruction that it could *be* a possible defense. Yet during the first trial, the jury had sent out a written question to the judge:

"What should we do if we think he was coerced?"

While the judge and lawyers were deciding what to do, the jury came in with a verdict: "Guilty." Rolando's lawyer was Earl Washington. Once, he had been a fine lawyer. But as he got older, he began to make mistakes. The *Chicago Tribune* ran a big story about the mistakes. How his clients, innocent, had ended up in jail. How had Rolando or his family even found a guy like Washington? I never knew. Anyway, it made me shiver to see his picture. You'd think the older you get as a lawyer . . . but that's often when you start to blow things. Remind me to get out of law soon.

Anyway, after Rolando was convicted, the public defender took the case on appeal. It took forever. For one thing, there's no money for appellate public defenders. It's not really clear why. While kids sit in jail and there aren't enough lawyers, the public defender's office actually turns money back to the county.

So it's amazing the boy's case was reversed. Coercion is not a very promising defense. And to be saved by a state court judge! Many of these judges aren't exactly Lincolns. And what's sad is, the giants in the law used to be in state court. Benjamin Cardozo and Oliver Wendell Holmes, Jr. came from the state bench. As late as John Kennedy, it was not the state but federal courts that had more hacks.

So what's the state bench like now? It's true that some states have great courts, but in Illinois, we elect our judges. A while back, a lawyer told me what it was like to go down to Springfield to argue in our supreme court. The night before, they have a big buffet dinner . . . well, I'll let him tell it:

" . . . It's a big catered thing. Silver spoons, white linen. If you want salmon, cold asparagus, it's all there . . . and the judges show up for it . . . and right on the buffet, they can pick up copies of the briefs in the cases they'll hear tomorrow, huh? So, you can pick them up like an hors d'oeuvre, a blue one, or a red one, whatever you want. . . ."

He didn't have to say these could be death-penalty appeals.

So if our case was reversed in appellate court, which by the way has no buffet, because the jury did not get an instruction on coercion, then maybe, on voir dire—

"We've got to ask them about it," Scott said.

I had an idea. I asked Scott if he wanted to hear it? My idea was:

"The State has to prove its case 'beyond a reasonable doubt,' right? So . . . what if it's an element of the case that Rolando was *not* coerced?"

Scott waited, so I went on:

"See my point? If it's an element of the case, then the State has to prove that Rolando was *not* coerced beyond a reasonable doubt?"

Scott waited for the point.

"So, my point is, why don't we ask the jury, 'Do you think the State has to prove every element of its case beyond a reasonable doubt?' "

Because then later we would argue . . . see, it's a trick question, in a way . . . because later we would argue . . .

I was whispering this very fast. Scott stared at me and said,

"I can't ask that!"

Oh. I see.

Well, what's their favorite radio station?

But Scott did try to ask about compulsion, so he went up to Judge K.: "Your Honor, I think you have to ask them about . . . 'Coercion.' "

Ms. M., the star pupil, corrected us: " 'Compulsion.' "

"Okay, 'Compulsion.' "

That's why we're all here.

"No," said Judge K. On voir dire, he would not single out one issue of law like this. "But I will say to them . . . ," and he paused, for effect:

" 'I will instruct you on the law and you will *follow* the law even if you disagree!' "

Scott nodded, but on the way back I whispered, "I thought a jury didn't have to follow the law!" Didn't I read that in Blackstone?

Not that I'd "read" Blackstone. But I'd read about this, I think, once, in a Saturday edition of *The New York Times.*

Now Judge K. called the first panel. Our jurors-to-be. If we didn't get twelve, we'd call a second panel.

Now in one big breath, the Judge went through what they'd hear at trial ("At-this-trial-you-will-hear . . ."). Well, I couldn't hear. But in the middle of this whoosh, out popped the word . . . compulsion.

I looked up. So did Scott. Did they hear? He said our little word: our defense! Over on the panel, I bet they didn't hear! So later Scott felt he had to ask a panelist, "Would you follow an instruction on 'Compulsion'?"

"OBJECTION!" said Ms. M.

"Sustained!" Judge K. said.

But still we had won a tiny victory! Now, in civil "litigation," if I won a tiny victory like this, I'd get to take a break for two months, but down here, at Twenty-sixth and Cal, the thing just kept going. Fortunately, as second chair, all I had to do was sit here and watch.

All that day I looked deep into the jury pool, and at the trophies fished up. Sometimes I thought I saw my own reflection. What follow here are my notes about some of our juror candidates. (I'm sure I have their numbers wrong.) Later, in a few cases, I have gone back to put in my second thoughts. Though I always wonder if it is wise to put in any second thoughts.

Anyway here are the notes:

Juror Candidate No. 1: Mrs. V.

I don't like her. She's East European, which I like, but it's in a "1938 East European" way, which I don't like. "Strike her," I write to Scott. Only, wait . . . she's smiling! Ah, so I think at least we should ask, "Ms. V., do you volunteer?" Why ask? Because if she volunteers, she must have a good heart!

And will acquit.

But she doesn't volunteer. But . . . would love to! Only she has to take care of her elderly mom. And her two sons. Two. They're grown of course. But . . . she's so busy, and . . .

STRIKE HER!

Second thoughts:

None of the panelists volunteer, so this could backfire. "Oh, they think I should volunteer, huh? Okay . . .

". . . I'LL SEND THIS KID TO THE CHAIR!"

Can't make her defensive, etc.

Juror Candidate No. 2: Wanda

"Ever been a victim of a crime?" the Judge asks her.

"I . . . I was mugged," she says.

"Do you know any victim of a crime?" the Judge says.

Wanda, after a long pause: "M-my father . . . WAS MUR-DERED!"

Excused.

Second thoughts, etc.:

1. Others wave hands, as if to say, "Pick me, my father wasn't murdered!" Or: "*My* apartment wasn't broken into." (That's the one I hear the most.) It's strange, too, the other ways people compete, like the woman who says, "Well, I have a friend . . . and her apartment was broken into!"

True for me, too.

In fact, I'm dying to tell people how my car was broken into. One morning I came out and in the backseat I found a homeless man sleeping. "Uh," I said, in a soft voice, "you . . . can't sleep in my car!" And he just yawned and walked off. (I admired this.)

2. I wonder if people like us, the juror wannabes, want to make a confession. It's weird to be so intimate this *fast* with a total stranger. They say that in Russia people can get intimate very fast, but that's a police state.

But then . . . down here, it's a police state.

Juror Candidate No. 7: Old Greek Lady

Since she's Greek, Judge K. smiles, is affable. But she has none of it. No English, see? No understand. See?

Though I believe her, Judge K. is pissed. Calls us up. "Now, I know she's been in this country twenty years and probably owns four restaurants in Palatine!"

He calms down. "But what can I do? I have to strike her."

And I notice how so many Europeans we see today . . . they don't speak English. You'd think, right now, in the European Union, the biggest export over here is: mimes.

Juror Candidate No. 9: Jewel

Can't read my note . . . oh, she's a teacher, black. The State strikes her. Good.

She reminds me of a black "Miss Grundy," like in the Archie comics. Scott wants teachers, but I'm frightened of them.

Juror Candidate No. 10: Principal

"No," I shake my head. "NO!" But he's a principal, and Scott says, "He knows what it's like to be fifteen."

(That's why we strike him!)

What bothers me: He's the headmaster type. The kind of "head" that haunted a hundred million British schoolboys. Turned them into novelists. Worse: British novelists. Anyway, the "head" is now staring at me like a boy he has to watch.

But Scott takes him.

But I'm watching this guy.

My second, etc.:

1. Why am I such an asshole about this guy?

2. I can't get over how, in picking people, I seem to have some real power. (Though Scott makes the decisions.)

3. By the way, Scott's rule is: "Pick nice people." Why? "In a big case I won," he says, "the jury came up later and said, 'Oh, did you pick us because we're nice?' And ever since, that's how I've done it." He didn't need pollsters, etc. (Well, he did, but he couldn't afford them.) And why is "nice" good? Because we, the lawyers, were nice. Or Scott was. And if the jury is nice and we're nice . . . then we can take on the other lawyers and cut their throats.

I'm kidding.

Seriously, it was the first time I'd seen Scott at work. A lawyer can seem charming, but this is not what Scott was like. He didn't try to seduce. Anyway, a seductive person is not nice. What made Scott dangerous was that he had the skill of a great trial lawyer and he really *was* nice! In a normal way. It's so normal it's not even a "style." So at first nothing seems to be happening. But at this voir dire, even the parts where Scott seemed to be doing "nothing," he was doing us a lot of good.

Juror Candidate No. 11: Mr. A.

Oh, Mr. A.! Rock on, because when Scott asks, "What's your favorite station?" he says, " 'XRT." Progressive rock.

"Progressive" for older boomers. This guy's a bit young. Long hair.

Even a hacker. Computers, etc.

Problem? Uh . . . he works with cops. "Yeah," he says, "they're like my . . . 'clients.' " He handles their computers. But the way he says "clients," it hits me:

He's saying it with a certain irony!

"TAKE HIM!" I whisper to Scott. Notice the irony?

But later I think, If the whole country's into irony, but we're slamming kids in jail anyway . . . why take someone for his irony?

But we "take" him.

Juror Candidate No. 14: Ms. Video

She "does video" and has a ball cap I'd love to knock off. Judge K. asks, "Can you be fair?"

Oh no. Someone broke into her car once. But she makes it clear: "You bore me." She yawns. Judge K. calls us up: "She just wants to get back to her 'Video'!" He's hurt: "I bet what she edits, it's TV, it's cop shows, trials like this!" I can tell, among the lawyers, our feelings are hurt too.

We don't mind losing the Greek lady, but this one's in television. Okay, let her go!

I just hope out in L.A., they knock off her little ball cap.

Second thoughts:

Suddenly, I'm aware of Rolando next to me. Out of a prison cell for a moment, what does he feel? Like he's been exhumed and unwrapped?

Widow of Naim? It's in Luke. Here's your son.

Rolando's mom is a few feet away, but it's creepy. I'm the one who sits next to him.

Juror Candidate No. 20: UIC

That means University of Illinois at Chicago, and this is a black undergrad. Lives with his mom. Scott shoves over a piece of paper. "It's a rap sheet," he whispers.

Which of our jurors were arrested, etc.

"Usually they don't give it," he says. "But they gave it to us, I don't know why."

As usual, I try to pretend I know what this is about. From TV, etc. But I've never seen a rap sheet. On the *jury!* If millions are in prison, though, it's only logical that people on our juries will have a rap sheet too.

"What's funny," Scott says, "is that on the jury questionnaire, no one admits to being arrested." Could this make it easier for juries to convict? "Oh, we've been to Siberia. It isn't so bad!"

Juror Candidate No. 25: Financial Analyst

He has short hair, but we take him.

Juror Candidate No. 28: East European?

Yes, another one. By the way, where are the Latinos? None. As I look at this woman, I have a troubling thought: Poles seem like aristocrats to me. Nietzsche wanted to be a Pole, and Jackie O's sister married a

Polish count, right? And in real life I fall in love with Polish women especially.

But when I see them in a jury pool, I want to strike them.

But this time I can't . . . she's . . . oh, red hair and . . . but she's married to a cop. This worries even Judge K., who leans in favor of the State a little.

"Given your husband and your brothers, who are all on the police . . . do you think you could be fair?"

"I . . . I would like to think so."

I melt. "Scott," I whisper, "we've got to take her." And then Scott looks at me. And suddenly I know: Am I mad? But that red hair! And she's a nurse.

"Scott," I say, "what . . . what if she's in pediatrics? What if . . . she takes care of children?" (I can tell this causes Scott to hesitate.)

"Okay," he says. And he asks, "Where are you a nurse?"

"Amtrak."

We strike her.

Juror Candidate No. 30: Juror from Hell . . .

Why? Because he's a white CEO in the burbs, but worse:

His dad owned a bunch of gas stations, which were held up all the time. So he probably has nightmares of kids doing holdups.

But before I can say, "STRIKE HIM!" Ms. M. says, "We strike him."

WHAT? I just gaped at Scott. Wh-wh . . . *what?*

Why did Ms. M. strike him?

"Because he's Jewish," says Scott.

I can't even begin to handle this. What? He's . . . what?

"It's not anti-Semitism," he says. "Ms. M. is Jewish. So is Mr. S. . . . It's just that the State likes to strike anyone they think may have a brain."

"But his dad owned gas stations. . . ."

But Scott explains: The State wants the weakest possible minds on a jury. They don't want anyone who might actually think.

Juror Candidate No. 32: The Italian

I knew this guy was dead meat, because he had a book. Another European, with wire-rimmed glasses. But the big thing is: He had a book.

A book with small print. Could be Gramsci, *Letters from Prison*.

Ms. M. strikes. No chance to save him.

Juror Candidate No. 35: Nice Person

A nurse, and she *does* take care of children. But there's a problem.

"I was abducted."

Everyone looks up. "Or . . . I was the victim of . . . an . . . attempted abduction."

Judge K. pauses, follows up: "Did you file a, uh, complaint?"

She nods. She's beautiful. "But nothing ever came of it."

What to say? Scott still wants to take her. But I'm now seasoned in this. "I think we have to ask, 'Who abducted you?' "

Scott looks annoyed. "What difference—?"

"What if it's an alien?" But actually I don't say this.

Her story may be a nightmare.

Juror Candidate No. 36: Even Nicer

Yes, this one is even nicer, but we strike her. Her husband is a cop. And a cop *in the military*. Judge K. asks her if she can be fair. With warmth, compassion, she says yes. She looks at us with a kind of love, yes, the kind that would have turned back invading Huns.

Again, I weaken. "Oh, Scott, we have to take her. . . ."

Fortunately I'm tied to the mast here, and Scott is steering the ship. NO.

I actually turn to Rolando. He shakes his head, furiously. NO.

My second thoughts, etc., about the women panelists:

The last one smiled! Ah, but what does that mean in a murder trial? A biologist did a study of smiles. It seems the apes used their smiles to tell other apes, "Don't worry, I'm harmless, see?" But since smiles were easy to "fake," the apes came up with something better: laughing. "I'm *really* harmless!" This biologist, a woman, did a little study. She had men and women watch funny scenes from movies. Like the orgasm scene from *When Harry Met Sally*. What did she find? Men laugh "loudest" when sitting with other men whom they know, their pals. ("Hey, bud, I'm laughing, so we're not going to kill each other, right?") While women laugh "loudest" when sitting with men who are total strangers. (Why? Unconsciously perhaps, she is trying to seduce or disarm the male stranger, make him more malleable.)

So in a jury room, if a woman smiles, it could mean "I like your client." But probably all it means is simply:

"DON'T MURDER ME!!!!"

So don't pick her for her smile.

Juror Candidate No.—God, I Can't Remember!

And don't we have TWELVE JURORS yet? When is this over? It's incredible, we still have to try the case. But here's the last guy I have a note on:

He's short. And from Dallas. Right there I'd strike him! "Wait," Scott says. The man is now saying, "I . . . I was charged once with a crime."

It's not on our rap sheet, so it's amazing he brings it up. "Th-they said, I . . . was stealing equipment."

I feel faint.

"I . . . I didn't do it." He stops.

Let him go! But now there's a hush. And Judge K. says, ". . . and?"

Another hush. "It . . . was dropped. But it . . . caused me a lot of worry."

So do we strike him? Scott says, "He *knows* what it's like to be accused."

But he's from Dallas, so we strike him.

Once a palm reader, who was ninety, said to me, "This line here says you are or *could* be a very nice person . . . but only if you stop eating meat." What would she think of me now, striking people?

I could go on with more notes, but they get garbled. It's hard to tell what was said by Mr. A., and what by Mr. Y. We were tired, but we kept going until we had our twelve jurors, as well as two alternates.

At last this was over. Then one of our alternates began to scream.

5. AN EERIE SCREAM

About midway through the day I had said to Scott, "You know, I can't stay for *all* of this, I'll have to go soon." And I shiver to think how he only said, "If you do, I'll be disappointed." So I felt angry, in a way, but now I had a rare sense that, yes, I had *done* something today. Like a child, coming home from school with a little drawing to show my parents.

When my cases don't go to trial, I don't have anything to *show.* "For us," says my friend Ed, a labor lawyer, "it's like ninety-nine pounds of input for every ounce of output." But here in one day, we had already picked a jury!

Now, let me say again, and again, that Scott did all the work. But still I had helped, and was proud of whom we picked:

They were nice, first of all.

Six men, six women. That was good.

Two blacks, two Latinos. That was good.

So now I'd saddle up and leave the trial to Scott. Good luck, okay? Seriously, I had work back in the Loop.

But now I felt awful. Besides, couldn't I just stay one more day, offer it up for Lent? It happened to *be* Lent, and I never give up anything, the way I used to give up watching reruns of *Magnum PI*. The idea of giving up food, or fasting, seems . . . beside the point. And I remember how a priest once said to our yuppie congregation, "If you all really want to give up something, why don't you all give up a day of work? That's what people in our parish are addicted to."

So I began to think . . . why not give up a day of work? And that was the moment I heard a shriek, from a woman, who was . . . just shrieking. . . .

It was the alternate, a Latino woman we had taken. She . . .

"What's she saying?" I said to Scott.

"I don't know."

"Madam," shouted Judge K., "MADAM, MADAM!!" And he couldn't stop her, and then the Judge was getting redder, and he seemed to be trying to think of a joke, but he couldn't think of one in time, and . . . oh no, too late. . . . Judge K. just exploded: "MADAM, YOU ARE ON THIS JURY!"

She screamed at him.

"No," Judge K. shouted, "You . . . Are . . . Not . . . Getting Off!"

She screamed louder.

"MADAM!" Judge K. had to roar. "I WILL SEE YOU HERE TOMORROW!"

Screaming, she stumbled out. . . . "What's she saying?" I tried to seem calm, as if, big deal: She's just warning us that we're all doomed. But the Judge was waving, calling us up, and when all counsel were around him, Judge K. was calmer, "Well . . . we won't see her to-morrow!"

We all still heard screaming in the hall.

"So," he said, "we'll have to go with only one alternate." It seemed to worry him. He was like a captain still in port and already had a sailor overboard.

After he found out more, Scott said, "That woman . . . she was on some psychotropic drugs."

I tried to joke, "Why should that disqualify her?" Still it was spooky: the way that, screaming, she would not join us in the ritual of this trial.

6. I CONFESS

Scott and I work in the same building, and it was dark when we got back. In fact, it had been dark all day. He went upstairs to work on his opening, and I went in to check my voice mail. It's odd, the almost libidinal pleasure of hearing that woman's voice, late at night:

"Your mailbox is full. Please delete unneeded messages." Which I do, because I'll do anything she tells me.

After this I took the elevator up to Scott's office and he opened the door and he had a yellow legal pad and said, "Here's my opening. Want to see it?"

"Okay."

He had written it in block letters. "Wow," I laughed. "This is really low-tech."

Though I like to print. The way the monks did long ago. That's how they saved Cicero's speeches to the jury. And Scott's speech to the jury was pretty good, too, but he wanted to work on the first line.

I had an idea. "Why don't you just hit his age, you know? 'Members of the Jury . . . this kid was fifteen . . . and in addition, he was fifteen . . . and in conclusion . . . he was *fifteen!*"

Except that now he's twenty-two. They may notice that.

"So," I said, "I'd say 'fifteen' three times in the first sentence."

Scott shook his head, but reprinting, he did say "fifteen" twice. "Well," said Scott, "want to read Rolando's confession?" He handed me a copy. Until now I've skipped over a little problem: that Rolando had confessed. Worse, he signed a statement, which I was holding. Worse still, he didn't say in here that anyone, any older kid, "made" him do it. Compulsion? Not a word. Okay, he was scared. But Ms. M. would tear into him, hold this. "See this statement? You said nothing, right?"

So . . . how to handle this on the opening?

Now, most of what I do as a lawyer is find an interesting way to tell a client, "Uh, I don't know." But since Scott himself is just a lawyer, I could say, flat out, "Uh, I don't know." Which I did.

But what to do?

I should have said, "Let's get a Story Consultant." At a wedding party, I ran into one at our table. He used to teach creative writing, but now he helps lawyers, he said, "to tell their stories."

"I didn't think they needed help," I said.

"Oh yes, they do," he said. "Mostly, I work on their opening statements."

Now, the old pros say that's where a case is won or lost. Of course the old pros also say this about jury selection, closing argument, etc.

"You lawyers," he said as he dug into his cake, "you don't know how to tell stories.

"I bet not."

"See, you don't realize . . . the jury wants the whole thing. In a story, with no interruptions. *We're* on the jury and we're waiting for you. . . . 'Tell us a story,' we say, and when we say 'a story,' we want you to go from ten P.M. to ten-oh-one P.M. . . . Do you remember how the lawyers *didn't* do this in O.J.?"

"No."

"Well, they *didn't*. They'd stop the story and get so caught up in the legal rigamarole. And lawyers. Instead of telling the *story,* you say things like, 'And then we will call Mr. X., who will testify that . . . ' Do you see?"

"I see, yeah."

"You can't interrupt the story."

Of course I am interrupting the story to say, I think this guy is wrong. To me, all lawyers do is tell stories, in just the way he said. My God, I wish they didn't. At lunch I can see guys, my friends even, wind up to tell me, for the hundredth time, the story of how:

Bank A

cheats

Trust B

over Land Parcel C.

"I told you this, didn't I?" Yes. But then they tell it again! It's their whole life, this "story." And since it's a civil case, and never settles, the telling of it can never stop.

And they can't seem to tell it to anyone except me, who's eating lunch.

What's *true,* though, is that lawyers don't read stories. It's too hard on our eyes. As my friend Father Grogan says, in legal and other work, we overload just one of the senses: the visual, our eyes. That's why for a lawyer like me a real story is too long to read. It is easier, eyewise, to read a single page of Kant than ten of Stephen King. But to Father Grogan I would say that "auditory," thanks to audio books, is coming back. I know a lawyer who drives to work just to "hear" a book. But it's odd how so many lawyers say they "read" them. So whenever a lawyer says, "Oh, I just read Homer," I wonder if I should ask, "Did you really *read* Homer? Or, as in Homer's time, just listen to him on a tape?"

But let's press the Pause button on Homer and go back to Scott and how he told Rolando's story.

By eight o'clock at night, he had an outline. And it did "go" as a story, in a straight line, as the consultant would have wanted, but it also lingered on certain things in a clever way. Oh yes, he told The Story:

How the big kids found Rolando.

How they dragged him along, to be a "lookout," at the backdoor of the bar.

How one of the older kids shot a patron.

How Rolando, terrified, ran away with them, etc.

But then came the odd part: Scott *played up* the fact that Rolando had "confessed." He went into detail . . . an odd amount, it may seem at first . . . as to how the boy was taken out of class and brought down to the station. How he had no lawyer. How this fifteen-year-old kid had to sign a statement late at night. And with little details like these, Scott was trying to answer the State's most powerful point, namely: If Rolando was forced into this, why didn't he say so to the cops? And what was the answer Scott gave in the opening?

Baloney.

Baloney and pop.

That's our case, baloney and pop? But that's what the cops had given Rolando when they grilled him at the station. And Scott has to do what a good writer does: not just "tell" the jury that the cops jerked around a kid with baloney and pop, but get the jury to taste things the way Rolando did . . .

The baloney.

The pop.

"Here, Rolando."

To see the way the cops were nice to him, he wanted to be nice back to the cops, to just say what they wanted to hear. So late on this night as we were in Scott's office, he told me, or put me into the scene, how Rolando had been picked up and taken out of class. And how he was only trying to please the adults.

And how did we know Rolando, like a good kid, was trying to please the cops, do what they wanted? He raised the "confession." Look, he said. Read it—and I did. "See," said Scott, and he'd point to a part. "See right here that he's trying to be a nice kid?" And Scott liked the story because he could show it in the transcript.

"Listen," said Scott, "listen to this . . . here, I'll read. . . .

" *'No one's forcing you, Rolando, right?'*

" *'Right.'*

" *'And have the police been good to you?'*

" *'Yes.'*

" *'And did they give you something to eat?'*

" *'Yes.'*

" *'What was it?'*

" *'Baloney sandwich and potato chips.'*

" *'And a pop?'*

" *'Yeah.' "*

Scott stopped, disgusted. Now can you taste that baloney and pop?

What kind of pop? I wondered.

"And," he said, "they let him make corrections! See . . . how he corrected their spelling?"

Carefully the boy, in the margin, had changed the word *taht* to *that*.

"See? He's trying to be a good kid," said Scott. And he told me how Rolando, at ten, had worked in a flea market. Always kind of a gofer.

"They do this all the time with kids!" Scott was fuming, now, about the State. " 'Oh,' they say, 'he didn't want a lawyer,' and they're telling him, 'Here, kid, just talk into the tape.' "

Scott paused. "Next thing you know, he's got a sentence of forty years!"

Of course, in Chicago, I should explain, they have nine-year-olds confessing. About a year after this trial, the blacks in Englewood blew up when the state's attorney announced that two little boys (ages five and seven) had confessed to what amounted to a *rape* murder! This turned out to be . . . uh, not the case. But if it were me, I'd throw out every confession without a lawyer. Oh, say some conservatives, you would let an adult confess without a lawyer present, wouldn't you? It's responsible to confess, it's "adult." Who needs to have a lawyer? We want to promote responsibility. When I confess, I'm most "adult." Bullshit. I mean, really. Look at Raskolnikov, who's cited in a new book, which I ought to read, on involuntary confession. At the moment that Raskolnikov is being most "adult" and confessing to an ax murder, he's also groveling, acting like a child. Pitiful. Compared with him, Rolando with his baloney and pop seems to be more adult.

In the end, who's more childlike, Rolando or Raskolnikov? I'd say . . .

Hm.

Rolando is, I guess. Did Raskolnikov sit there changing *taht* to *that?*

I told Scott, "Good night."

Yeah. Okay. Tomorrow, he said, we'd start at ten o'clock.

7. MY NIGHT AT BOB'S

It's odd how in my life, after being young so long, I'm now the oldest person on the El, at least when it's after eight o'clock. Tonight I'd meet up with Bob, a lawyer, and have dinner at his house, and forget about tomorrow. That night I told Bob how Rolando was fifteen, etc., and Bob said, "Forty years," and shook his head.

I now blushed, as if I had spoken of something I should not.

How happy, tonight, not to have an opening to give tomorrow, or have to do a trial. Of course, like everyone, I still think, "Oh, I'm under so much stress." Tonight on the El, I'm sure all these kids, the bankers, etc., they all think they're under stress.

In the Freshman Union when I was eighteen, each night I'd pass the guard and envy him. "How happy I'd be if I could go home like him tonight and just watch TV, and not have to do this paper on . . . the Puritans!"

This was 1968, when my hero Robert Kennedy would die, and he used to say, "Men are not made for safe havens," and while I admit it has a little existential kick, especially to a freshman who's eighteen, I have always believed, deep down, we *are* made for safe havens. I spent the 1960s in a safe haven. No doubt I still feel guilty. To think that while other kids were burning down ghettoes, or small villages in Vietnam, I was so . . . safe, I could have slept through it. Fire a gun, etc.? Unimaginable. I was from Saint Xavier High, and when you're from St. X. . . . well, as the girls in the other Catholic high schools said, "It's like dating the son of an ambassador." (It wasn't.)

But even though I was from a safe haven, I knew I was for Kennedy. Even when everyone but me seemed to be working for McCarthy, Eugene McCarthy, who ran to stop the war. It was he, not Kennedy, who deserved my support, since *he* wanted me to be in a safe haven. I recall him saying in *Time*, about his daughter, "The best thing she could do at her age is just to be in *college!*" That's why I disliked Mc-Carthy, because I thought this way too. While Kennedy, my hero, would be rash enough to pull us *out* of college. He thought one good way to stop the war was a universal draft.

So I wanted a safe haven. But I also wanted Kennedy. This might have been the start of a little lifelong tic. E.g., yes, I want to settle everything. But at the same time, shouldn't I go to trial?

But I want to tell everyone who graduated from college in 1976 or 1980 or 1983, you missed very little by missing out on that time. Because if you were like me, then you'd have been in a safe haven, in which nothing would have happened. For while it's true you could get cancer like in *Love Story,* your life is set up so that nothing can go that wrong. That's why it's hard for me to grasp a Robert Kennedy. When the world is so wonderful, why would he do anything to throw it all away?

That night I tried to tell Bob: After seeing this kid in the cell, I have to get him out. On the other hand, I don't want to lie awake all night over it either, and if I had to do this the way Scott does, I'd be dead at forty-two . . . not so easy either, since now I'm over fifty.

The thing that now gets me about Kennedy dying at forty-two is that, in a way, he was murdered so quietly. It's like a door swung open a little bit, and poof, the guy was gone. Everyone expected it. A friend of mine had a nightmare, and woke up at two A.M., and turned on the radio . . . Kennedy had just been shot . . . well, you knew it. But in a certain way, he's still around, in a way you and I won't be, after we try to live in a safe haven, but in the end have to die anyway.

And so as usual I had a nice dinner with Bob, and was glad to get home early. Thank God tomorrow I wouldn't have to do the opening. I wanted to "help" Rolando the way I wanted to work for Kennedy.

It's a terrible thing, I know. I love to second-chair.

8. CALVIN: INTRODUCTION TO . . .

Why start so late, at ten A.M.? Poor Judge K., he had to let us vote. Today, Tuesday, was the Democratic primary, and it was also Saint Patrick's Day, so in Chicago this was like an eclipse—or two Christmases falling on the same day. As I say, we elect judges. As I hurried through my ballot (I have to get to court!), I had to vote in thirty or so judicial races! Who were they? Didn't know. My God, this'll take longer than jury selection! And I have no one like Scott next to me to ask, What do you think?

I always look to see if a friend is running for judge. Usually, a poor guy just trying to get out of law practice. But who wouldn't want to? The other day I ran into a woman who was now a judge. "What's it like?" I asked.

"Oh!" she said. "At last, I feel like I'm doing something with my law degree!"

"Can't do much with it as a lawyer," I said.

"Oh, *that* job! That's impossible!"

Now *she,* I know, had just been restless. But other lawyers run because . . . well, they start to get the shakes, can't even read a court file, etc. So a few friends help them run for judge. We all think, If I can pull my buddy out of the trenches, then maybe, with a stretcher, they'll come back for me!

So every time I get a ballot and go to the judicial races, I like to see if I am running.

I noticed today that I was not.

Because the trial started so late, I could stop by the office first. By 9:30 A.M., I'd even dictated four letters. In days when lawyers had two martinis at lunch, I suppose this would have counted as "a whole day's work." So when I flagged down a cab . . . I was still using cabs to get to Twenty-sixth and Cal . . . I felt, Well, at least I got in a "two martini" day.

When my cab pulled up and I'd paid out my twenty bucks(!), it seemed at first the whole courthouse was empty: as if there'd been an act of war, not just an election. Room after room: empty, empty. But way up on the sixth floor, in a single room, there was Judge K., alone of the judges, and fuming.

It seemed we had a juror missing. "Maybe," someone said, "he's out voting, Your Honor." Looking for your name, Judge, on the ballot.

(Judge K. happened not to be running.)

Anyway, while the Judge ordered a guard to do a search room by room, Scott said to me, "Let's go back and see Calvin."

I didn't want to, in the least.

Calvin was the older kid who'd done the murder. He was seventeen then. Why shoot? Because at the bar, some old guy, tipsy maybe, was too slow to hit the floor. And because Calvin had fired, Rolando was in prison, more or less for *life*. Well, that's the curse of felony murder. Some guy like Calvin fires, and if you are anywhere nearby, you're just as guilty too. It doesn't matter if you're fifteen, or didn't have a gun at all. It only matters if a guy like Calvin forced you to come along.

As we walked, Scott was saying of Calvin, "You'll like him, he's a nice kid."

And while Scott said this in a nice way, he didn't use the same tone of voice as when he'd said, "Rolando is a nice kid." In a way, it seemed Scott said "Calvin is a nice kid" as if to warn me.

After all, this kid was a killer.

So I knew I wouldn't see him in a golden light. No, just the standard-issue county light, which always had the color of urine.

Urine, which inked into all five of my senses: The urine light I could see, the urine I seemed to hear trickling down the walls, the urine I could smell, the urine that I could taste or feel coming off my skin after I was back there for five minutes.

That's the light I saw Calvin in at first, and I didn't think he was innocent. No, all I could think was, This kid is beautiful.

Now, for me, it's a first to talk about a *man's* beauty. But I'll just say it was male beauty of a standard NBA kind. Or the kind that Leni Riefenstahl, in her post-Nazi photos, might have taken to, and but for a certain scariness, Calvin might have been in jeans and staring from the back of GQ magazine.

Now I remembered what Scott told me, the night before, of their last talk together: "I said, to him, 'Calvin, you come across as mean, but you're really a nice guy.'" (Scott was referring here, in part, to Calvin's offer to testify.) And then Scott went on:

"'No,' he shook his head, 'I'm not a nice guy . . . because if I were a nice guy, I wouldn't have done this to Rolando.'"

Scott was coming back, to make sure Calvin understood something. He was going to be our whole case, but. . . . This was the first time he would say, under oath, that he had "coerced" Rolando. In doing so, he took a risk.

"I have to warn you," said Scott quietly, "because your testimony on this is 'new.' What you're saying is new, I mean. . . . And they could come after you for perjury."

I tried to see Calvin's eyes, but it was like a veil had dropped down.

"Now, I've never seen it done," Scott went on. "But they could do it."

He wanted to make sure Calvin knew: perjury. Because even Calvin might not be in here forever. It was odd, I now thought, how wonderfully he had grown up in here. Though Scott would never have said, Prison-is-good-for-him, he did say to me, "Calvin's the kind of kid who does well in prison."

But to grow up in here, in a dungeon! In the Middle Ages, big families used to bring a youngest child or two to a monastery or convent to "grow up" in: as an *oblate.* In Latin, it meant "an offering to God." And now, in a way, we have "oblates" to the state. We bring them in at fourteen, fifteen.

And then to add perjury? To be trapped here even longer?

Anyway, Scott seemed about to say more, but no, he didn't. Then Calvin seemed about to speak . . . but no, he let it go. As Scott and I went out, I said, "Wow." No idea what I meant by "Wow." But Scott nodded as if he knew, and he added this:

"But out on the street, Calvin was . . . I mean, he's not in here just for a single murder . . . he held up a couple of pizza places."

By now, a deputy had found the lost juror, who, it turns out, had been wandering the empty building. So what is the next thing, procedurally?

Now we go!

Go?

Yes, go, like "All hands!" And: "Rig the boom," and . . .

Except in state court, this goes even *faster.* I mean Ms. M. just stood and began . . . talking. Wait, aren't we going to pledge allegiance, or something? Did we just start? I have tried cases in federal court, and I don't recall . . . well, just starting. Whatever we "do," we don't just . . . start.

I think I was upset, because I wanted to think about Calvin. Because it hit me in the holding cell that when I was eighteen, and eating in the Freshman Union, I'd been . . . introduced to another Calvin. To John Calvin, to Calvinism. This is what I came to major in. Maybe being in Boston drew me into Puritanism. But I began, like a moonie, drifting into it. I should have been reading Vonnegut, but the Puritans had a lot to say in the 1960s to kids like me. Righteousness. Justification. And most of all . . . the Wrath of God. Even *Grace* was a terrible word: For if you have it, you're free. . . . It means you're above the law.

And because it was our special grace to Stop the War, we seemed to be above the law. For if we could burn our draft cards, fight the draft, what law, if any, could now apply to us? In a way that's what Calvin said. It so freaked me out, I think it's why I went to law school.

I'm a lawyer, I believe in the law. But some kids break laws and end up in the elite. And others break laws and are stuck in prison forever. Never getting out.

The year of this trial now starting, how many kids, ages fourteen to seventeen, went into the state prisons of this country?

Over 7,500. It's easy—for them—to believe that there is predestination.

9. OPENING

Coiffed, in pearls, Ms. M. sailed into her opening. The strange thing is, she could have just "read" it from the transcript of the first trial. In a way her opening was truly "written out."

Scott gave me an old transcript. I forgot to follow along. While she changed it, of course, it would be hard to blame her if she thought, I can do this like before.

Same opening.

Same witnesses.

Same direct.

But this had a risk, because our case had changed. For one thing, we had Calvin. We'd do more on coercion. So if they stayed with a script, we'd be trying improv.

I'd like to try a case if I could read it word for word. But Scott could set some traps as he knew where she was going.

An example: In the first trial Ms. M. would talk about the baloney sandwiches, to show how nice the State was. This time she did this even after it was clear Scott would use baloney too.

It was an odd opening, because Rolando barely showed up in it. First Ms. M. talked about Mr. Lyons, the victim. Then she went on about the evil Calvin. And only at the very end, way at the end, did she even say the name "Rolando." I bet the jury wondered about that.

Actually, I bet they didn't. But I'd talk this way to myself, in my head: Oh, I know we scored one here. Yeah, I bet the jury is wondering about *that,* etc., etc. So Ms. M. began with the man shot at the bar. "'Little did James Lyons know that night as he blah, blah. . . .'"

Oh come on, this is corny! The jury isn't going to buy this—

The trick was to say something *at all* about him. He had no wife. He had no relations.

He had no phone.

Another strange thing: Though he was a regular at Mitch's Place, the bar that was held up, he lived in Villa Park, which is quite a poke away.

But nobody knew him. And he had no phone. And there was something so numbingly "not there" about this guy that halfway through her opening . . . even Ms. M. seemed to forget him. This is a terrible thing to say, but at least we had a victim that nobody seemed to know. All Mr. Lyons had left the world was a single scrap of paper, a state exhibit, a medical record:

"Lyons, James F., 17 W. 505 Manor Lane, Villa Park, M/2/56;

Gunshot to Rt. Side of Head." And farther down: "GSW, entrance above right ear."

GSW. Calvin put the gun there: Pow.

But later I felt, Isn't it worse to kill a man who had nothing? Didn't even "exist"? I thought how Mr. Lyons drove night after night from Villa Park, far away, to sit in a bar where no one knew him. He didn't seem to be a drunk. Wasn't it worse to kill *him?* I remember a reader's letter to a column by Mike Royko. It was a letter from a reader who complained about a column about when the city should shut the bars. Oh, Royko had said, if you can't get drunk by one A.M. you've really got a problem.

Wait, said the reader, I'm one of the guys who sit in bars at two A.M., at three A.M. Think I'm doing it to get drunk? You see, since my wife died, I'm all alone. At night I can't sleep, and a bar, at three, a light is on, there are people, and I can . . .

I can go somewhere.

Royko ran it, without a wisecrack. From what is said of Royko, I wonder if maybe he wrote that letter to himself.

Anyway, at last Ms. M. got to Rolando. How he was in the back of the bar. Watching. While Calvin and another boy (who they never caught) was in the front. And then she got to the very worst part:

As the customers lay on the floor, the testimony will show that the defendant, one Rolando, etc., *did take or lift the wallets or money from persons lying on the floor,* etc. Oh, I wanted to burst out, but Calvin made him do it!

But it made me wince.

I know, there are "two sides to every case," or so it is for block-heads with no imagination.

Now Scott rose. At a podium he spoke softly as if to an elder. He spoke, without notes, just as if he was in his office the night before. He didn't give a "Speech" the way Ms. M. did. Nor did he tell a "Story" as if . . . well, they were children. He was just being himself, I realized. Now in Trial School, the older lawyers say:

Be yourself.

Usually, it's bad advice. Even when I'm not being a lawyer, it's hard to be myself. But Scott in an eerie way really is himself. And for Rolando, this was a good thing, because I could see now, the jury was going to like Scott. Now in the first . . . oh, minute, which seems to last forever . . . it might seem Ms. M., shouting, was more polished, but then I thought, No, this is going to be good.

Because a trial lasts for more than a minute, it's for days, weeks, and just as an actor can interest people by "doing nothing," I think a lawyer can devastate by "being normal" and "a nice guy." Ah, it's the hardest thing in the world to do!

By the way, in the first sentence I think Scott said two, or even three, times that Rolando had been "fifteen." And Rolando, as if embalmed, still looked like he was fifteen. Of course the jury would figure out, Didn't this happen seven years ago?

Anyway, even if we can't argue "Human Rights" in an American court, at least we can say . . . hey, the kid's fifteen! Scott sat down and I wrote a note, "GOOD OPENING," and Ms. M. called the first witness.

10. DIRECT AND CROSS

The first up was the bar's owner, "Patricia." She'd been tending bar that night. Scott whispered as she began, "Here's the transcript."

From the first trial.

"What should I do?" I said.

"See if she says the same thing as the first trial."

Uh . . . I guess she left out a few words. I wondered if Ms. M. had let Patricia read it over. One good thing for Rolando: Now she was hooting about his age. "Oh yes, the Hispanic boy came in. . . . Well, I KNEW *he* couldn't buy a beer!"

Shows he's young.

Her husband followed. He forgot some of his lines too. I had a sense that he and his wife didn't care about this case now.

Rolando, upset, passed me a note: "The middle juror is sleeping!" Yes, the "UIC" kid. Passed it back with a scribble: "But the others are AWAKE!" (I thought.)

Two witnesses down. So we took a break. Now came the cops. To whom Rolando had "confessed." "Would you like to do a cross?" Scott asked.

"You want me to cross-examine the cops?"

Maybe because both were Irish, he thought that I, being "Irish," would know their ways. No, far more likely, he, Scott, wanted to save his every neuron cell, every muscle fiber—both the "long" fibers you need for a marathon and the "short" ones for a sprint—for the uphill to come: a cross of a former state's attorney, and then "our" direct of Calvin, and then of Rolando too, and of, really, the whole ordeal, right up to the jury instructions and the closing. It's not true that a trial is a marathon. At points, it breaks into sprints!

So couldn't I do a cross of a cop?

Now, a nonlawyer may wonder, "But isn't a cross harder than a direct?" Oh no. No.

No, it's vastly more draining to do direct and "disappear." It's always harder "not to be there." Since it means being *everywhere,* as God is. (Or just in two places at once, like Saint Martin de Porres.) Ask what's harder: to be a piano teacher backstage as your five-year-old pupil is tinkling for a crowd in Carnegie Hall, or to be the critic who gets to razz the kid? As coach or teacher or, really, the "auteur," you have to "lead"the witness . . . but also the jury, the judge, even the opposing counsel a little. And the only rule you have to follow? You can't LEAD. I hate direct. It takes hours and hours to make it sound unrehearsed. Then the witness you have to coach, but can't coach, can't remember the biggest line. You have to pour telepathically the answer into their heads. Come on, say it, say it, please God, say it!

While cross? Comparatively that's easy. Take "Patricia." Okay I might have gotten away with:

Me: Uh . . . when you say, "I knew he couldn't buy a beer," you knew he was pretty *young* . . . DIDN'T YOU?

Patricia: Yeah.

Me: Ha. Well . . . no further questions!

See? Not so hard. But direct is like taking a steam bath, one of maybe three in a row. So if Scott's only asking me to do a cross . . . I decided to calm down, and I thought it over, and took a deep breath, and smiled, and said to him:

"No. . . ."

No! "Scott, I don't know the file!"

Okay, he said. He let me sit.

But he gave me advice on "How to Sit with Rolando." "You want to sit," he said, "so the jury can see that Rolando is 'Part of Us.' You've got to pull him in."

"How?" I said, like a guy at a tennis lesson.

"You know, lean a little this way. . . ." (toward Rolando).

Poor Rolando. I noticed he had had his hands over his mouth. Should I tell him? Or let the jury see how nervous he was?

Anyway I tried to sit closer, and when the jury came back, I even tried to beam telepathic thoughts: "See? I'm sitting close. . . . He's Part of Us!"

I kept beaming, as if I were on. But Scott had to do the cops. They were two big Irish Catholic guys, who made me think, again, of when I was eighteen and living back in Boston.

11. COPS

Later that night, after he did the cops, Scott would say to me, "I . . . I don't really like Saint Patrick's Day."

I didn't press it.

Out on the street, it was raining, like an industrial accident. I had my own views. It's a "Day" that long ago began to give me nightmares.

Now I had a new one: Lieutenant B., Detective M. Oh, come on! How bad were they really? I've had darker Saint Patrick's Days.

And they made me think of them.

They made me think of being a kid Rolando's age, and living back in Boston. It was a shock, when I was eighteen, to be Irish and come to a place where the Irish were working class. In Cincinnati, I thought they were all lawyers and judges and had Protestants for maids. But in Boston they weren't just working class, but a mean, bitter-in-the-Belfast-acid-rain working class. Violent. Went chasing after black kids, and beating them bloody.

And they were the servants! It was a shock to see old men, who looked like my wonderful grandfather, handing me my towel as I walked into the gym. In the dorms, of course, I knew several Irish Catholic kids, who often made a big deal, too big a deal of it, and to one of them I said uneasily, "You know, I'm half German on my mother's side." Looking around, in a lower voice, he said:

"Come on! We're *all* half German on our mother's side."

Okay, I was naive.

And when I walked past townies in Charlestown, I could even wonder, You know, it's possible I could be mugged . . . by my own people! Or I would have wondered that if I'd ever had the nerve to walk around Charlestown. Remember, back then, there was still no such thing, commonly, as the Guinness/Harp "Irish" bar. Back then a really Irish bar, as my friend Tony said, was a plastic kind of place, which maybe just had Bud, and the way you knew it was an "Irish" bar was that if you knew where to look in the jukebox in the back, there would be one—just one—single, Bing Crosby "45." Ah . . . like finding the entire Book of Kells.

All of Boston was so gray. Full of Coolidge banks that looked like prisons. It's odd to think that if I'd grown up there, it was theoretically possible to have gotten in a lot of trouble. I could have been mean. Really mean. As people get when they are as poor as the Irish were. God, it makes people mean.

Remember the book *How the Irish Saved Civilization?* I know how. By being too small and weak to invade anybody else.

Even in a big country, they could still be mean. I remember how a monsignor years ago told me about the meanness of the American Irish: "Saint Patrick's Day? I don't want to hear about it! Look at the Jews, how they buy bonds, and give money back to Israel. And in Chicago? Oh we sing the songs, but to the Irish back home, you think we'd ever give a dime?"

But all along I knew, Okay, I'll knock the Irish, but it's kind of an act, and any moment . . . I'll fall back in their arms! For that's part of being Irish, too. And maybe this was the year I was about to, until the moment that Ms. M. called . . .

Lieutenant B. and Detective M. So why did she call them? I guess it was to press the jury: Rolando had confessed. And to show how the cops were nice.

And big.

Nice and big. This was at a time, as I said, when the cops here had just gotten a five- and seven-year-old respectively to confess to rape (and murder). And this year had the usual complaints of police abuse, even torture. There are more abuse complaints about Chicago than New York police. But the mayor, as I heard him quoted on public radio, said this was really a good thing. Why? Shows that in Chicago, unlike New York, people have a sense of freedom, they aren't afraid to complain, etc.

Only a healthy city could have so many complaints of abuse, or even torture. Now, I say "torture" because that's what some of the lawyers, and reporters like John Conroy, say. My neighbor R., a criminal lawyer, used to talk. On the El to work, he'd tell me about a certain cop who had tortured his client. "He'd take off his captain's coat, put on his sergeant's stripes."

Now poor R. himself is dead. Killed by his own son, mentally ill, out of an institution. When R. was stabbed a block away from me, and the cops came rushing in, R. begged them not to hurt the boy: how his son was out of his mind, etc.

Friends said, "That's R., being the lawyer, right up to the end, pleading for his own killer."

The Pope has a line: You can't let death and darkness have the last word.

So first up was Lieutenant B. Very Irish face. Brian Dennehy, the actor. White, puffy. Eyes shut.

His inner Irish child waiting for a stroke. Of course that's a shitty thing for me to say, but what a thing for this guy to be setting up a kid.

B., up there, would close his eyes. The suspense was: Would they open? Ms. M. asked things to show that Lieutenant B. hadn't tortured Rolando or anything, and that in fact he gave the kid a pop.

Scott came up to cross. B. opened his eyes. Then shut them.

"Did you read the Miranda rights?"

"Yeah."

"How'd you read 'em?"

"How?"

"Did you read them off the card?"

"Naw, I have 'em memorized. Or maybe I did use a card."

"Show us."

The eyes, which had been closed, opened. He showed us.

And for a second or so his real face floated up. I *heard* it break the surface: pish.

Then he shut his eyes.

"Was there a Youth Officer?"

"Yeah."

"Why is there a Youth Officer?"

"Because. He was fifteen."

Eyes opened; but no face floated up.

"You got him out of class?"

"Yeah."

"Freshman?"

Eyes closed again: "Freshman."

And it was so still that as B. stepped down, it seemed . . . that somewhere, a coin dropped in the box, then Bing began to sing.

But how Rolando was shaking! Not at B.: no, he was staring at the UIC kid, who was out and out SLEEPING! Judge K. too was staring, getting mad. And when Scott came back, even he said, "I heard him snoring." Being a populist, I sort of defended his right to sleep. Besides, we'd known he was in *college,* hadn't we? But if I had been Rolando, and in *my* agony, would I want anyone around to sleep? But the UIC kid had an unnerving way of blinking open his eyes, and then for a moment, unlike B., he'd be eerily *awake.*

Anyway, Detective M.

Also Irish, puffy, over fifty-five, but far, far more overweight. I wrote Scott a note: "THIS GUY . . . SMARTER THAN B.!" His weight, by dragging down his body, seemed to free the mind to rise. Scary the way he'd made himself a wreck.

Yes, and a wreck can be dangerous. Better sail around.

Scott went up to cross.

"You were at the school on December first?" "Yessir." "Went in the class?" "Yessir." "Read him the Miranda rights?" "Yessir." "Give him a pop?" "Yessir."

Now, in Trial School they say, Get the Yessirs first. Then go for the Nosirs. So now Scott went for the Nosirs.

"Didn't call anyone? Public Defender?"

"Nosir."

"His mother there?"

"Nosir."

"Any lawyer?"

"Nosir."

"Youth Officer?"

"Yessir."

Yessir? That one woke us up! The Nosirs to me were sort of like white noise.

But it was White Noise from White Males. I wonder what the women on the jury thought. Detective M. was so one-note he seemed to hypnotize himself. Yessir, Nosir, Tick, and Tock.

Unconsciously, he began to show how oaflike he must have been with Rolando that night. And Scott just led him on.

Didn't Ms. M. see what Scott was doing?

Yessir, Nosir.

I didn't know Ms. M. had a witness who was about to flip things on us later.

When they closed their eyes, what were Lieutenant B., Detective M., seeing? They *saw* something, and if I could cross them off the record, I'd loved to have asked, "Detective, when you shut your eyes, can you tell us what you're seeing?"

Maybe it's . . . oh hell, I ought to leave these guys alone.
Who's next?

No, we took a break. I liked how in a break Judge K. kept on working. He'd call up lawyers and do status hearings in his other cases.
Maybe he thought, today, Since I'm the only judge in the building
. . . someone has to work!

Everyone was out campaigning. It was odd, because Cook
County state court is America's biggest court system. Or so I read.
Most judges, etc. So here I was, at the O'Hare Airport of Courts, and
it seemed as if there were only a single room where planes were taking off and landing.

This break, I watched Judge K. take a plea.

A man, about thirty, was standing there as the Judge mumbled
through the criminal acts, and I could only catch a few words:

A guy, thirty, was pleading guilty. Judge K. droned on with the
particulars of his crime, but I could catch only a few words:

" . . . torture her . . . then mutilated her body in . . . then with
premeditation. . . ."

Did everyone around here have to mumble so fast?

The mutilator's P.D. was looking away, shuffling papers and trying
to seem busy. Sure. Real busy.

I remember up in the holding cell, with Calvin, Scott had made
that remark: "Your lawyer, I bet he didn't have the time of day for
you." And Calvin had said nothing.

But in this case, could you blame a P.D. who didn't have the time
of day?

Anyway, Judge K. had now stopped, and I guess it was the defendant's turn to speak. I guess. It was hard to tell. The guy who did the
mutilating seemed bored, matter of fact.

Nor did Judge K. pretend to look at him.

Anyway the guy who did the mutilating said, "I'm . . . sorry." It could have been sarcastic, hard to know. He shrugged a little: "What can I say?"

No one looked at him. He said, again to no one, "I'm . . . sorry."

It didn't look as if the cops had tortured this guy. You wonder how that kind of thing is decided.

Okay, break over.

Everybody refreshed.

Now Ms. M. called the worst witness, though thank God in the wrong order, in the middle, not at the start or end. It seems that night, two brothers, Latino, had been drinking when Calvin and Tim (the boys with guns) said, "Get on the floor." Here's the bad part:

The two brothers said a third kid, i.e. Rolando, came over to them and frisked them.

Here's the weird part:

"Gold," not money, is what the boy wanted. In the first trial, the first brother claimed Rolando had said, "Give me your gold!"

Come on, I thought, no one says that, except in *The Treasure of the Sierra Madre.* But at the first trial, that's what the first brother claimed Rolando said.

At this trial the second brother testified in his place, but he agreed Rolando had said, "Give me your gold!"

On cross Scott asked, Did the witness's brother *have* any gold?

No, said the second brother. That's why he figured Rolando had meant to say the words to *him*.

Q: How did you know it was *Rolando* if you were facedown on the floor?

A: (smile) When he asked for my gold, I must have looked up! We took a break.

12. MEET THE AUTHOR

Time for lunch. I told Scott, "If you could get a decent lunch here, I'd do this every day!" Since I was only second chair, lunch was the part I dreaded most.

The jury rose, and Scott and I wandered out to the elevator . . . and getting in behind us was Judge K. in a blue blazer! My God, were all three of us going to dine at the Gangbangers Lounge? In federal court, this wouldn't happen, ever, that I'd be on an elevator with a judge! For a moment I thought:

Would I buy the guy fries or something? Might not be ethical.

The Judge was rather chipper. By the Gangbangers Lounge, he stopped and said, "Did you ever read the book *The Bonfires of the Vanities* [sic]?"

"Not the movie!" he barked, as if he thought that's what I understood. "The movie, with Tom Hanks, it's AWFUL! But the book, you know where he says . . ."

Here Judge K. waved his arm: ". . . how this place, *here* . . . it's the *Center of the Universe!*"

I smiled, nodded.

But I didn't want to eat the food.

But now the Judge went off, and Scott told me, for the first time, the courthouse had a cafeteria. They had albacore tuna and everything. So we began to walk over.

Though the court had been empty all morning, now the people were coming in. A dozen lawyers, P.D.s, a few cops, were passing, and they'd say:

"Scott!"

Or: "Hey, Scott!"

And now I was more worked up than in court, because the people saying "hi" pumped me up: I bet this is what it's like to be a lawyer on television.

For Judge K. had said, "This is the Center, etc."

I could catch the chitchat of lawyers at the Center of the Universe. Like:

Judge Z., is he on the take?

Is the mayor in bed with the Mob?

Now, that I don't believe.

Well, you should believe, a lawyer tells me. You think, he says, because he denounces the Mob . . . ? They all denounce the Mob. In the Mob, they don't care if you "denounce" them. You're no good to the Mob unless the People think you're clean.

On, and on. From books, I already knew a little of how they talk at the Center of the Universe. But my God, I'm out of it. What can I say? I don't know how anything seems to work.

Oh, you don't know if you bribe a judge, you have to bribe a state's attorney, too?

No, things are that corrupt?

Oh, it's not like it used to be!

If only I could stay down here and take an intensive language course! Meet for lunch with some lawyer every day who has prepared a little lesson from . . . that day's "metro" news, which I flip through without comprehending, but which they can decode. If the billion bits of Chicago newstype in all the papers can be sequenced in just the right way, it will lead to the key, which in turn will unlock the Big Secret of the City. By which I mean the Secret that tells or lays out what the Original Deal was, from which every later Deal is descended. It has something to do with the Mob, but I don't know what. They wouldn't even tell Capone when he came out here. Certainly, they won't tell me. They figured, being a civil lawyer, I'd run off and tell some woman judge in federal court.

In fact, when I'm in this cafeteria, I notice other lawyers will switch subjects and talk to Scott about their houses:

"Hey, Scott? What's this I hear? I hear you're moving to Oak Park?"

"Yeah."

Oak Park is a suburb. Safe for your kids. But it's also an easy drive to where your clients are in firefights with the cops. So the P.D.s and ex-P.D.s like Scott tend to live out there. One of them was going to handle Scott's closing. It became clear to me as he talked that he had been Calvin's original lawyer.

"Scott," I said when he left, "isn't that guy . . . Calvin's lawyer?"

"Yeah."

"But you said to Calvin, 'Oh, I bet he didn't have the time for you.' "

"He was a P.D.!" said Scott, defending him. "He had a million cases!"

Earlier, we had met Jack, the one P.D. down here I know. In Cincinnati, he'd gone to Elder High, a rival of St. X. And he grinned at me: "What are *you* doing down here?"

That is, what is a St. X. guy doing down here?

"I'm helping Scott," I said.

Jack had once asked me for an opinion, as a labor lawyer, whether the P.D.s could continue as a union. Jack was then the head of the P.D.s' union, and a court had declared that a union of lawyers was illegal. The rationale is that every P.D., even in bond court, is like someone in "management." My opinion on this didn't matter. The union, legal or not, kept going anyway and has gotten decent raises. A P.D. in felony trials can make . . . $70,000 a year. Not bad.

Just about the state median for *all* lawyers. Except, he may also do

four (as in *FOUR*) *death-penalty cases a year!* "You know Sam Adams?"
Jack said to me once. "The defense lawyer?"

"Yes," I said, because I felt I should.

"Adams says no one should do more than one death-penalty case
a year. I'm doing four!"

Anyway, after he got over his shock of seeing a Jesuit-educated
lawyer here, Jack asked us what our case was about. Scott told him,
and said, "He was only fifteen . . . only now he'll seem a lot older to
the jury."

"Where's he been?" said Jack.

"Prison, seven years."

"That'll age you."

Jack turned to me and grinned. "These are the kind you hate . . .
it's the ones where you have a chance." The way he smiled, he seemed
to know I had no idea what I was doing here.

Ahead of me in line, Ms. M. was drinking a glass of water. So I
guess the water is okay, I thought. So I began to fill a glass also.

Then I stopped. Now that I was in line, it hit me: What am I
doing? I have work to do back in the office!

I have heard of people having attacks like this, and now I had one:
I've got to get back to the office!

I've got to phone the office . . . NOW!

And then Scott came up with his tray and said, "Let's go sit
with Rolando's fiancée." I caught my breath. I was okay. And now I
began to wonder where Rolando himself was having lunch. In his
cell?

So we took our trays and sat with the fiancée. At another table, I
noticed, Ms. M. was now drinking some of the cafeteria's coffee. So I
guess the coffee is okay.

Yes, calm down.

"This trial," I said, "it's going fast."

"Yeah," said Scott. "*Now* do you want to do a witness?"

"No."

Then Scott got up and said, "I have to meet with Rolando," so now it was just me and the girl. I say "girl," but she was a manager at First Chicago.

Look at her, I thought, with real shame. Is *she* in such a panic to call her office? I wondered how she had told the bank, "My fiancée's up on murder." But it was nice to think that in the Business World even now, she could get off a day for this. Once or twice I'd longed to ask Scott, "If at fifteen Rolando went to jail . . . I mean how could a girl so pretty, and a bank executive, be his *fiancée?*"

But I suppose before there were any banks at all, or commercial paper, or holders in due course, young women like her had come down to courts like this to wait for their young men. Mayan. Aztec. Colonial Mexico. Why should a job at the bank change this ritual for a young woman? I get sappy about women, except when I see the *National Enquirer, Star,* etc., in the groceries, and I realize how dreadful they really are.

As we sat, she went back to reading her novel. It was something by John Grisham. This irked me, and I wanted to say, I suppose our trial is not as interesting. But in a way, she'd have the right to say, Speaking only as a reader, I'd like to know . . . *What is so interesting about it?*

So for ten minutes I watched her read. Maybe I should have brought a book. Which?

Oh, my old "Nutshell on Criminal Procedure"? No. Back in my criminal-law class, even my professor said, "You can learn just as much reading *The New York Times.*" It's not true. Yet I'd slept through O.J. Why did this one interest me?

Two reasons:

Nothing legal, in law school or later, is of any interest to me, except when suddenly I have a client.

Also, criminal law seems too "cute." I hate myself for liking the "cuteness," the talk in the cafeteria, etc. In our culture, haven't we had enough of this drama?

Left to myself, if I had been given the idea for a movie like *The French Connection,* I'd have turned it, in a month or so, into a piece for a law review. As a civil lawyer, I need something like this to read. E.g., how so much of "Twenty-sixth and Cal" violates, say . . . human rights. Just the fact that everyone in a holding cell is black or brown. Doesn't this violate something we must have signed as a treaty? Yes. Of course. (I found out later.) It's the Convention Against Every Form of Race Discrimination. A treaty that somehow, incredibly, even America signed.

This Convention prohibits anything, such as a Twenty-sixth and Cal, or any system that, regardless of our "intent," ends up clobbering, unequally, one racial minority or another. "Oh," we say, "we don't mean the drug laws, death penalty, to apply unfairly. . . ."

Sorry, no excuse.

Isn't that what we should be putting into novels, and even on TV?

So I don't like the way it seems "cute" down here. It's the same way I feel when I'm reading a novel, etc. And look at this girl, right now, what she's reading. I can't bear it!

Oh come on, lighten up. Everyone likes a murder. What should she read?

Before I take back my tray, I'd just like to note: Jane Addams of Hull House used to work down the street. Of her many books, out of fashion, one is *The Spirit of Youth and the City Streets* (1909). Back when she had an Oprah-like buzz, she campaigned to set up the first juvenile court so that kids like Rolando would not be tried down here.

At the turn of the century, people used to read her books. They talked of Jane Addams for president, even though as a woman she couldn't vote. Then, except for *Twenty Years at Hull-House,* all of her books went out of print for years. Yet once in this very neighborhood, she was bigger than Mother Teresa: Right now, I was standing in her Calcutta.

I mention her because her great belief was that, one day, in the world, we should live under a system of international law, of treaty rights, of human rights. She talked this way when no one else did.

She even talked this way during World War I, which she opposed. The country was enraged. She was America's sweetheart. How could she be against the war? Poor Jane Addams never recovered.

I know how easy it is to chide her, as some of her own biographers do. Where are these international courts? Where is this new legal system she imagined?

Poor Jane Addams, she'd be shocked if she came down here and saw, a century after Hull-House, some of what is going on.

Yes, where are these international courts? I don't know what to say. But as naive as it sounds, I still think she is right, and Kant is right, and that somehow by our very nature, as a species of rational beings, we are moving to such a world.

But in the middle of a trial, at Twenty-sixth and Cal, a subject like this is too depressing to discuss.

13. THE STATE "RESTS"

As I ran back, I found out that Judge K. was really mad! He called us up. "Well," he said, "we've got a juror back there, and he's telling everyone that he knows someone in Rolando's family!"

He shook his head. "Well, let's keep going. We'll bring him out here when we're finished."

I didn't know what to think. But I tried to look upset.

Before resting, the State had two last witnesses: (1) the coroner;

(2) a woman state's attorney who had taken Rolando's statement at the station.

First came the coroner. Scott had said the night before, "Remind me to stipulate to her testimony." But I'd forgot. It turns out this is an excuse to let the jury see a photo of the dead man, Mr. Lyons. Ms. M. had to bring over the photo, to let us see. She waved it in her cheerful way: "Oh, go on, look at it! It could be a lot worse!"

I looked. Mr. Lyons, his eyes shut, seemed as if he was playing a game and about to smile.

The coroner, who at first was olive (East Indian), went white on the stand. It may be a trick coroners have, regardless of their race, to go whiter than a powder pancake as they testify. She didn't say much: just how the bullet entered Mr. Lyons.

"Any ideas?" said Scott as he got up to cross. I did have an idea: to ask how close Calvin was when he fired the bullet.

"What would that show?"

"If it's close, it means Calvin *is* scary." Which would prove Rolando was right to be scared. (Say, I may have a gift for this!)

So Scott asked, "How close, etc.?" and the coroner shrugged. "I couldn't say." So Scott cut it off.

Ah, I was mad! If she'd only said . . . I, I could have been a hero.

Now came Ms. H., the State's last witness. Last: a relief. Except, as I should know, the last is lethal. Ms. H. is she who would "nail" Rolando. For at midnight when the boy confessed, she was the assistant S.A. on duty.

So pretty: so I thought, as she came up to testify. It's what many a boy at fifteen might have thought that night: "Wow, she's so nice."

Now she was back, to put Rolando back in prison again. The job of Ms. H. as before was to say, "Yes, this is his confession, the one I took." No doubt the jury would like her. As before.

Then she'd read from what was a "Q & A" with him.

Now at first Ms. M. proposed that Ms. H. would read her part and Rolando (albeit twenty-two now) would read his own part on that night seven years ago. So Ms. M. walked over to our table. Oh, would Rolando like to read?

"Let me," I whispered. I'd acted in high school, and I could make Rolando sympathetic.

"No!" said Scott. "We can't be seen to take any part in this."

He was right, of course, but I thought how . . . I'd put a tremble in my voice . . . no, don't try it.

By now, many times, I'd read over the confession, the Q & A. So in my mind, as I "heard" it, it no longer seemed so bad.

To hear it aloud was a shock. Ms. H. did both the "parts," hers and Rolando's. I will skip printing out the two or three pages of this long Q & A. In a childlike way Rolando tells . . . well, *a* story. It was the one Ms. H. wanted him to tell.

" '*Q. Did you meet with Tim?*

" '*A. Yeah.*' " ("Tim" was the name of the other boy, never caught).

" "*Q. What did Tim say?*' "

In baby talk: " '*Oh, Tim wanted to go and hold up a bar or something.*' "

And on like this. At first, Rolando had said no. Then Tim came back, and he said yes.

Now of course I knew (any lawyer knows) a client—*a child*—can give you six versions of the same story. Every one is true, and none is quite what happened. So I could nod, and think, This is consistent with what "our" story is, etc.

But Rolando in his Q & A says nothing, not a word, about Tim— and Calvin—forcing him to go along. Also, I was trying to put myself in the scene, at the station, with this very pretty woman, at midnight, after spending all day with two big oafs. What story would I tell?

Still it sounded different out loud. I just prayed—which is odd for a lawyer, I know—that the jury would listen to the parts I listened for. Especially Ms. H.'s question, right at the end, when she asks what he "consumed."

The "A" is:

" 'A. Baloney sandwich, two pops, and a Snickers, and some potato chips.' "

Then Ms. H. is done and reads, " 'Let the record reflect that it is now eleven-thirty P.M. on December 1, 1990. . . .' "

I much preferred the Irish cops.

Cross?

Now, I'd have gone up to shout at her, and made everything worse. But Scott was a pro. He went up, he was cool.

What marks a pro is not having to Win It All, every time. He knew our turn would come. He worked at bringing out our case. . . . He "did" the baloney, the pop.

He let her be nice.

It was the simple, calm way he made a dent that made me think, I could never do this. Do what?

Do nothing. Or not too much.

Be calm.

Sit down, when it's time to do that.

But when Ms. M. said, "We rest," I wanted to jump. Ah, now I was in a panic, and I had another attack. Again: I have got to get out of here and call the office. What, be calm? I . . . no, I had to get out of here.

And of course there was a break, and I ran out to find a phone and call the office. I now knew the State was winning, and I wanted to hear someone say, "Your mailbox is full."

That is: Come on back up! We need you!

But she who never fails me said, in a disapproving way, "You have no messages."

Impossible? NONE?

But weeks later I realized, Maybe the "message" was I had no messages, so just go back there and sit down.

When I did, Scott said, "We start with Calvin, right?" And he went off to get Calvin from his cell.

14. NICE GUY

Two things as a lawyer I forget.

Don't give up. Ever. What Churchill, in his old age, said to the students at Sandhurst.

And on direct exam, stand as far away from the witness as you can. Because the witness should now be the only one the jury's watching.

That's what Scott did with Calvin. "You're in prison clothes," he said. "Can you explain the sentence you're serving?"

A chair squeaked. Mine, damn it.

"I'm serving forty years."

I was moving my chair to see him. Like the prow of a ship, the Judge's bench was jutting out to block my view.

"Do you know the defendant?

"Yes," Calvin said.

He said it in a way that could stop a beating heart. Maybe it did stop the heart of . . . well, the beautiful juror who had said she'd been abducted. By now I'd moved my chair so I could get a view of him. After Calvin said, "Yes," I remember his next words, not an exact transcript but as I scribbled them on my pad. . . .

"I put a gun to his head," said Calvin, "and I said, 'I'll kill you.' "
Quote. Unquote. Period. Pow.

What I now admire most is how Scott disappeared. Except that Calvin was so *great*. He knew just how to frighten, yet underplay it, too. For example, take the part where it's after the holdup. The boys are running, etc. And was it true, as Ms. M. had said, they split up the money with Rolando? It was true. Calvin gave Rolando forty-five dollars. Aha! But now Calvin said, "I made him take the money, to make sure he shut up."

"What did you say?"

He spoke as if a burning coal had touched his lips: " 'Here . . . you take this. Take it! And you better not say anything!' "

Scott, far away: "And?"

"And I took my gun, and pointed it."

So how could the jury convict, if "beyond reasonable doubt" meant anything? If ever there's a software program for Guilty Beyond Reasonable Doubt, the jury's PC would have to kick out Not Guilty. Right?

Scott sat down. On my pad, after putting "WE WON!!!," which I underlined in felt tip, I think I added: "GREAT!!"

Scott always slipped back, like a scout on a mission. I thought we should have a parade! Okay, I may not know criminal, but I know a good witness. I wish I could have yelled up to Calvin: Kid, you're a natural. You've been in prison seven years? You can handle yourself on a stand better than Bill Gates does (ever see the video of his dep?), or better than a Bill Clinton, and while you're scary, yet—

Wait.

It's bad when a lawyer falls in love with his own witness. How often I do this when "I Bring a Case for the Poor."

Bad.

Once a lawyer on the other side, with real pity, said, "I feel sorry for you, you have to believe your own clients." But it's not that I believed Calvin, I just liked him as a witness. If I seem a little ga-ga, it's because *he talked in quotes.* What do I mean by that?

On the stand a bad witness will say:

"I threatened him . . . uh, the defendant." But Calvin, being a master, would go:

"I said to Rolando, 'Rolando! I'll blow your head off!' " *Not:* I think I said that maybe. . . . No, it's: Quote. Unquote. Bang.

Who knows his exact words? He puts you in the scene. That's all the jury wants. And later, on her cross, what can a lawyer like Ms. M. say? Ask him about his use of an exclamation point after "Rolando"?

Now, since Calvin would have intimidated *me,* I expected Ms. M. to shrink a bit, but instead she seemed to race up to and spring on him.

"He's your friend, isn't he?" (Answer!)

"No." (Cold.)

"You're trying to protect him, right?"

Calvin paused. He would make her go at his speed. "No."

Meanwhile I'm sighing as loud as I can like I'm an Al Gore and Ms. M. is a Bush. Why? Because I'm unnerved, like Gore! What unnerved me is . . . Ms. M., who should be beat, is . . . smiling! Now, on cross, unlike direct, the lawyer comes up very close. In her pearls and coiffed hair, she was close, smiling. She picked up a transcript: "I want *you* to read . . . to the jury . . . what *you* said to the police." And Calvin, I knew, had said nothing about coercing or pulling any gun on Rolando.

Calvin—had to read this?

"Objection," said Scott. "Side bar."

Out of hearing, Judge K. said, "Basis?"

Scott could keep Rolando from reading in Ms. M.'s "play" because Rolando has a right not to "speak" under the Fifth Amendment. But since Calvin was not on trial, he could not cite "the Fifth." So . . . what was Scott's "basis"?

"Prejudicial," Scott said.

"Yes," I now spoke for the first time. "Uh . . . extremely prejudicial." I thought that was a better argument.

Overruled.

So Ms. M. now handed Calvin his own words to "read" aloud. She would "read" the questions. She was smiling, and I thought, Oh, poor Calvin. Ms. M. began reading: " 'So you ran out together?' "

Calvin, reading: *"Yes."*

Ms. M.: *"And you each took your share?"*

Calvin, reading: *"Yes."*

And not a word about pointing a gun to anyone's head. Yet as Calvin read, something mysterious happened. Instead of Calvin tagging along with his sheepish yeses, he seemed to be the one cross-examining Ms. M. Each time he said, " 'Yes,' " in the reading, he seemed to be saying: " 'Yes,' *but why don't you ask me why I just said, 'Yes'?"* And the longer it went on, the more Ms. M. seemed to be . . . evading Calvin.

As second chair I tried to beam this insight to the jury. I bet the woman who'd been abducted felt that way too.

Alas, though I scoffed at the time, Ms. M. did score a point on Calvin: "Well, since you're in prison now, *you can say anything!"* Which was untrue, as she must have known. Calvin was running a risk. But Scott could hardly ask, "Oh Calvin, by saying all this, don't you risk being prosecuted for perjury?"

Not to mention kidnapping.

Yes, a good point for our side, but how could Scott do that to him? Back in the cell, I had wondered why Calvin was doing this.

Was it because, as Scott said, "Calvin, you're a nice guy"? Maybe in prison Calvin kept seeing Rolando, and it was unnerving him. No, not likely. Or maybe he never saw Rolando, and this unnerved him more. Or maybe when he became an adult, Calvin decided to become "accountable."

Or maybe he was just curious. An experiment, out of boredom, to see if he could get him out. (This is how I talk because, lately out of boredom, I've been rereading Dostoyevsky.)

Whatever his reason, when he stepped down, he had beaten Ms. M. Well, arguably. (In law, how else would he beat her?) As a guard took him out the door, I thought, This is the last we'll see of Calvin. Now he'll disappear for forty years.

Scott said later that Calvin'd been lucky to get forty. "That was 1991. He'd get a lot more today." By his late middle age he might get out. I know a local of the laborers where they clean out the sewers, and a lot of the guys are like Calvin, wading down in the shit.

Should he ever get out, that'll be his job. If he's lucky.

15. A CRY (PART TWO)

As a deputy went up to the Judge, I saw it was near five o'clock. Come on, Judge K., let us go home! But that morning he'd said, "Ladies and gentlemen, we work a full day here. And by 'full day' *I mean we go to six P.M.!*"

Now I saw his face going red. Then came a cry that could have iced every star that makes up the Big Dipper. *"What?"* He went even redder. He said, *"what? . . . to the JURY????"* Just then I'd been in a reverie about how Calvin did okay, and how being on trial was not so bad, was it? And how cool it was that a guy like Jack, though from Elder, had come by our table. How I even wanted to call Ms. M. now by her first name. What had I been *afraid* of? Then . . . screaming, I just heard screaming! And Scott ran up. So did Ms. M. We could hear the deputy, repeating the whole story: "Yeah, Judge, there's a juror back there, and he's been telling everybody just like that. He's been saying, 'I got to talk to the Judge 'cause I gotta get off this jury. . . . ' " The deputy stopped. I guessed this juror must be the nut we'd heard about before.

"Yeah, he's back there," said the deputy. "Saying how, 'I live in this kid's neighborhood. . . . Who knows? He's got friends who could come looking for me. . . . ' "

"And what," cried the Judge, "did the *other* jurors say?"

"Judge, they said, 'Look, don't worry,' or 'Maybe you should talk to the Judge.' "

Judge K. couldn't speak—except, he could: "He said this to *THE JURY???!!!*"

By now up in the Big Dipper the last star had turned to ice, and even Scott had gone pale. Ms. M. was shaking her head. Everyone but me knew what this meant: *mistrial*.

"He's tainted the jury," someone behind me muttered. Ms. M. was already checking her calendar, to see when we could do the "re-trial." Scott went to check on Calvin. "I was going to send him back tonight." Downstate, to prison. "But now I have to keep him here."

No! We had to do this over?

And at that moment Judge K. was waving: "Bring him OUT HERE!" And now the deputy brought out the nut, whom I'll call "Mr. D." He had a big fat stupid look of a certain type of man, a plumber or cop, who "knows," oh yeah, exactly how things work. "Yeah, I know, pal."

Out he came, fawnlike as Bambi . . . for a second, I trembled for him.

"Sir," Judge K. started softly, "could you tell us . . . what your concern was back there?"

Mr. D. shook his head. "Judge, from the very beginning, I could see where this thing was heading. . . ."

"And where was it 'heading'?" said Judge K., but it was hard to hear him.

"I mean . . . 'developing.' When I heard where this bar was? That's my neighborhood. It's two miles from my house. So . . . I'm thinking, like, I could run into this guy's family at the Ace or the Jewel."

With a big fat look, he went on: "So, I said to the others back there, 'I got to see the Judge!' "

"The 'others,' and what did they say?" said the Judge, and we were quiet.

Mr. D.: "They laughed."

They'd laughed. You fathead, they must have thought. But Mr. D. said, "They said, 'Don't worry,' but I told them, 'Yeah, but I got to live in that *neighborhood.*' "

What "neighborhood"? He lived two miles away. In Chicago that's like another world. How could anyone from Chicago think that was his neighborhood?

And now, thank God, the Judge could go ka-boom: "SIR!" Pause. "MR. D., SIR, YOU DO NOT KNOW WHAT YOU HAVE DONE!"

Mr. D. said, "Am I excused?"

"ARE YOU EXCUSED? ARE YOU—?"

And they say that in space no one can hear you scream. But I believe you could have heard Judge K. say:

"YES, YOU ARE . . . *EXCUSED!!!*"

And as he fled, the Judge said to no one in particular: "If anyone wishes to file for contempt, I'm willing to entertain it." That would be a headline: JUROR PLACED IN CONTEMPT! It's hard enough to get someone to be a juror now. Yet that cry, from Judge K.! It was for a waste of his two days. But what about us? There is a famous quote that nothing is more depressing than London on a Sunday afternoon. But what of a Sunday afternoon before a trial? Now Scott, Ms. M., and yes, me, if I came back, would have to face another one.

At that moment it felt even worse than a Sunday afternoon. Tomorrow, alone, what would we do? The Judge stared at Scott. "I suppose," he said to Scott, "you'll move for a mistrial." Then, half to himself, Judge K. said, "Certainly we'd at least have to have some individual voir dire." He meant we would have to ask each juror, one by one, if the juror felt "tainted," and if even one said yes, we'd have to start over.

Ugh.

"Okay," said the Judge, "tomorrow we'll try to figure out what to do."

16. AND WE WERE WINNING!

Ducking into Scott's car, I said, "Ah, and we were winning!" (But did I know?) "Let the State . . . let Ms. M. move for a mistrial." (Why would she?) Ah, and Calvin had been so good! Now, what irked me was, next time Ms. M.'d be ready for him.

And I wouldn't see it. I mean, I'd already blown two days.

Ah, damn it!

Scott turned on public radio, for the returns. "I wonder," he said, "do I go home and watch the returns . . . or do I work on my closing?"

"I don't know."

It must be nice, I thought, to work on it with your wife and kids downstairs. If I had to do this at night, I'd also want to have a wife and, uh, kids.

Deadly quiet kids.

It kept raining, and then minutes later I said, "I think we should go forward."

"Look," said Scott, who was driving, "we can't decide that now. Tomorrow, we have to talk to the jurors."

"Yes, you're right."

And now we were stuck, under a bridge. "What do you think will happen . . . I mean, tomorrow?"

"I don't know," said Scott. "Nothing like this has ever happened before."

"You think we should move for a mistrial?"

"I think we have to poll the jury."

And over and over, because we couldn't move, we said the same things. What should we do? I don't know. Think you should work on the closing? Yeah. Isn't this traffic awful? It's bad. Yeah. It is. Why aren't we moving? Somebody's stuck. What do you think Judge K. is going to do? I don't know.

It's strange how two lawyers, like a married couple, will drive themselves nuts by saying the same things over and over. Every minute or so, Scott or I would say:

"You notice how Mr. D. said, 'The jury laughed'?"

"That's interesting."

"Yes, that is interesting."

Scott drove me all the way home. I felt guilty. He was the one who had to work on the closing.

And that night I didn't watch the returns. And the next morning I didn't look to see even who had won for judge. Now, that's a disgrace, because at one time I was on the board of the Chicago Council of Lawyers. I was on a panel that screened judges and gave out our endorsements to the voters. But then I dropped off the panel. Went back to thinking, So what?

Even now, when I could see up close how much difference a judge makes, I still couldn't work up an interest in who'd won.

It's a big problem for the Council!

It was started under the Old Mayor Daley, and back then in the 1960s, even many Big Firm Partners wanted to change the world. Stop the racism in our city. Now I guess there aren't any, or at any rate, no one cares. Or maybe no one has the time. . . . This was the year that Kenneth Starr, the Special Prosecutor, was chasing Clinton to impeach him, and no one even had the time for that. I had gone to a friend at the council and said, "The Council should have . . . a town meeting or put on something about this . . . you know, a seminar, or something. . . . 'The Clinton Impeachment: What Role Have We as the Legal Profession Played in Creating the Crisis?' Let's discuss it, you know?"

"It's a good idea," said my friend. "But I can't think of a time of day they could have it."

Lunch? Too busy.

Afternoon? That's work.

Evening? People want to go home. If they're not working.

And if we don't have time for a panel to save the President, who's got time to go down and help Rolando? No one has three whole *days*. There's not even time now to go "Ahem!"

Again, Clinton/Starr is a good example.

Long ago, when the Big Firm Partners, like at Paul Weiss, etc., still had time to read the papers, they might have headed off what a Kenneth Starr was doing. ("We don't prosecute a sitting president, for civil perjury, in a deposition, in a case that was dismissed for failure to state a claim.") There was a time when even a few of the biggest Partners could have gone, "Ahem." And Starr would have had to stop.

In the 1960s, the Big Firm Partners also had time for cases like Rolando's. That's why I went to law school: to be that kind of Partner.

No, the reason I went is that I'm the oldest of six kids, and the oldest always goes to law school. But strange to say, I did dream of being a Big Firm Partner, and doing pro bono on the side. I used to think of which of these private clubs I would join:

Hale and Dorr

Cahill and Gordon.

Yes, the dues. I'd start out as a busboy, but one day I'd be running the Club. I'd be one of the club's many-ringed sultans, and time would dangle from my fingers. For the sign of my power would be my time, or leisure. It may have been small even in the 1960s, but time has all been relative since at least 1910, or whenever Einstein was able to quit his bank job. And remember, in law school all we really learn is not the law, or where law is, but one skill really:

To work, *always.* Otherwise, as lawyers, we'd have no skills.

So to have any time is to have colossal power. To be emperor in the desert, how much water do you need?

Yes, they had time.

Now I laugh, because I know they have no time. And the Partners who were giants now seem to me like dwarves. Yes, how smart I was to be in a firm that is too small to be a Small Firm. But then a year ago, when I heard a judge speak, I realized I might be wrong.

Judge Tatel is a Clinton man, on the U.S. Court of Appeals, and I heard him at a rare luncheon for lawyers. They sold a lot of tables, but very few people were there. Too bad, because Tatel speaks in Edward Gibbon–like sentences that either he memorizes or reads from Braille, because one of the things that gives him power as a speaker:

Judge Tatel is blind.

At lunch he spoke of the Big Firm Partners of the 1960s. He went through his own career. He had done it all. Worked full-time as a lawyer for a civil rights organization. Though Judge Tatel is white. Then worked as an associate. Then as a Partner in a Big Firm. And while it is fine to be an outsider, etc., to bring justice to America, "we need the Partners in the Big Firms."

Not the associates. The Partners. The Big Ones.

Then he spoke of civil rights in the 1960s, and men like Ed Rothschild. While I had no idea who Rothschild was, Tatel shamed me into thinking that I must know him, somehow. He told what Rothschild and the other Big Firm Partners did after the cops raided the apartment and shot to death Fred Hampton of the Black Panthers. "Right after this, we met in Ed's office. Right there Ed drafted a letter to the attorney general, and we all signed . . . calling on Mitchell to investigate."

Imagine: to call up Mitchell about the Panthers!

But now in Big Firms all pro bono is falling, and fast. In the 1990s, pro bono hours dropped from fifty-six a year, already low, to under thirty-five.

At my table I thought, "Tatel's right." Indeed, as a kid, I'd been right: that only as a Partner in a Big Firm could I bring any justice to my city. I knew more when I was young! If I go down to Twenty-sixth and Cal, what's that going to achieve?

Zero. I'm from a Small Firm. Even if I'm "there," I'm not there.

But these guys . . .

Ah! But the suspense of Tatel's talk was this: "Does he 'see,' in this banquet hall of the Hilton that there now seemed only fifty of us in the room?"

Or there were, till I had to go. I also have work to do.

17. MY THIRD DAY OF TRIAL

Though I was exhausted from my two days as a second chair, I knew I'd be thinking the next morning, I'll miss taking these cabs to Twenty-sixth and Cal. I'd miss being there, with Scott, and Ms. M. and the P.D.s, most of whom seemed to wear Navaho blankets, and I'd miss feeling . . .

Pure and undefiled.

Because we were doing something serious, and it seemed to me that the lawyers down here were like people who had sold all their worldly goods, or even our very birthright, which was to drink Starbucks in the Loop and go into a Borders at lunch, just so we could do this serious thing, far away in a place uncontaminated by the world. So it pissed me off when the cabbie, in the cab I took today, just *had* to flip on "Doctor Beth," who's a sex therapist and has a call-in, and all the drive down, while I was trying to be pure and undefiled, there were callers like the young woman who called in to say:

"Doctor Beth? When my boyfriend and I make love, I have the strongest desire to urinate. . . . Is that normal?"

"Can you turn that DOWN?" I had to shout from the back. Then, looking out at the boarded-up bars, I sighed. Sad, how it has to end in a . . . mistrial.

I was glad that Twenty-sixth and Cal, after the election, was full and noisy again, and when I found Scott, he was chatting with a P.D., a guy who had run for judge. If you do a death-penalty case, as I said, you can kiss off being federal judge, but who knows, down in state court, the voters might vote you in.

The P.D., who seemed shaky, was still waiting for word. "I'm ahead by five hundred votes," he was saying, to no one in particular. "And there are only a hundred and fifty precincts left to count."

I could have guessed he was running for something. Unlike a normal P.D., he wasn't in a Navaho blanket, or even a poncho, but had on a blue suit and tie.

"Poor guy," I said to Scott, "he's really nervous." And all that day I noticed him going from court to court, and I could hear him saying the same thing, over and over:

"I'm ahead by five hundred votes . . . there are only one hundred and fifty precincts left to count."

I never knew what happened.

Now out came Judge K., and he was the old Judge K. again. It was as if the night before he had weakened and even seemed to pity the defense, or Scott at least, as if we could decide if we wanted a mistrial. But now, this morning, that was all over. Now it was he, Judge K., the Judge, who would decide. (Yes, I, and I alone, will decide if this idiot, Mr. D., contaminated *my* jury!) And Judge K. would do this by calling:

Juror No. 1

Juror No. 2

One by one, each one, into his chambers, or private cubicle, and ask each juror, face to face: "Are you tainted?" By the idiot Mr. D., blithering how Rolando's pal might find him at the Ace? And one, only one, juror had to blink and say, "Uh," and we, on the defense, would cry, "Mistrial, Your Honor!" Though he, Judge K., would decide!

Now, at this moment, Ms. M. waved Scott over and whispered something to him. When Scott came back, he said, "She's offering . . . twenty-eight."

Twenty-eight?

"Years?" I said. (Yes, idiot.)

"Yeah," said Scott, "but . . . he's served seven. So he *could* be out in twelve, so it's really five more."

My God, I need a calculator. Then, to my shame, a demon in me now would mutter, for the whole case: "Hey! Is it really worth *your* precious time, just to fight over five more years?" Because after all it's . . .

Five more *years.*

Well, Scott said: No.

No. Of course, that's right. But her offer was now gone. That was a shock for me as a civil lawyer, where we can dither over an offer for two or three *years.* But in big civil cases, the settlements cover:

money
injunction, or institutional change
reprisal clauses
legal fees

But down here, as Scott said later, "The decision tree's a whole lot simpler. 'You want five years? I'll give ten.' " And he might have added that an offer like Ms. M.'s has the half-life of an isotope, and you have to decide now, or poof, it's gone, and you end up doing twenty years. As a civil lawyer, I must say, the whole thing gives me nightmares!

"Okay," said Judge K., as Ms. M., Rolando, me, Scott, etc., jammed into his "office," which was only a little bigger than the backseat of my car. "Call in the first juror!"

Now each juror came in . . . one by one, alone . . . as if each one, separately, had to go across a rope bridge. It was neat how Judge K. handled them, since I had expected he would blow up: "DIDN'T I TELL YOU PEOPLE NOT TO TALK ABOUT THIS?" But no, with each juror he smiled, waved:

"Come on in!"

Uh . . . the juror's face was like a child's.

"Yes, come in! Sit down!" As if the Judge was pouring tea.

True, Judge K. being nice like this at first was scary. Then it hit me

that our Judge at one time had been a lawyer. He knows how to handle, how to put on a witness, I thought.

"Now Ms. Q.," said the Judge, coming to the point after much
charming banter, "you know Mr. D. And he has been excused.
Hmm? And . . ."—he paused to smile, in a fatherly way—"and *you
know,* don't you, that you aren't supposed to discuss the case . . . ? "

And Judge K. is smiling at her.

" . . . Hmm? *You* know you have to wait to hear all the evidence,
don't you?"

And Judge K. is smiling. We are all smiling.

And Ms. Q., the juror, is sort of smiling, but mostly (I think) she's
going to burst out laughing. (Come on, Ms. Q., please don't break out
laughing!)

"Now," said the Judge, "did you have any conversation with Mr.
D., or hear Mr. D. say anything to anyone?"

Ms. Q. nods. "He said, he . . . was worried he'd run into someone who knew . . . the, uh, 'defendant.' " She tries not to look at
Rolando, inches away, staring like a big bird at her.

"Well now," smiles the Judge, without really smiling, "did you
give that *any* consideration?"

(Ah, the mark of a pro. On a transcript, bare, does that look like a
leading question?)

"Oh no!" says Ms. Q., and her eyes are shining, as if to say, Isn't
that the right answer?

Then Judge K., smiling, is the gallant: "Oh, Ms. Q., thank you,
and would you be so good as to send in the next juror?"

As each juror came in, and the Judge did his Would-you-like-cream-
or-lemon-in-your-tea routine, I kept thinking, Isn't this something,
to have the juror . . . up close and personal, etc. . . . . thirty-six or forty
inches from *Rolando?* It seemed every juror made a point of *not* looking, but in a way that tried to say, Oh, I know where he is.

How could Rolando be allowed up this close? And after a while I was staring like a big bird at *him*. Sometimes I looked over at Scott, then at Ms. M., to see if they were staring at Rolando . . . no, they didn't seem to care.

The fifth, sixth juror came in. "Now, you didn't . . . ?" Everyone smiling. Many of the jurors trying not to laugh. And then, by juror number six, I decided, Sit between Rolando and the juror. Why? So the juror, a foot away, would not feel "threatened." So I moved my chair. *Wait!* If my client's innocent, why would I move my chair? Okay, so, squeak, I moved it back. And then . . .

What was I *doing?*

Oh, God, when I think of that poor boy, I could give a cry.

Meanwhile, with each juror, Judge K. said the same words, and after the first one, Scott had even said, "That's perfect, Judge. Just keep saying it like that."

"Ah!" said Judge K. "Now I can't remember what I said!" But only one time did he go off script, and then Scott frowned and said, "Oh, Judge, that wasn't really as good."

During this I decided that as "second chair," I should try not to squeak, but look very closely into the face of each juror, and do it steadily, and with love, as if to say:

I love you.

And: By the way, look . . . see? All of us, the Judge, Rolando . . . all of us are friends now. . . .

Ah! Didn't I think so? We were like a team. Me, Ms. M., Scott. I felt like we had opened a small Chinese restaurant and were inviting people in. And I knew this: Even if by a miracle I were to do another, or a hundred criminal trials, never again would I get to stop halfway through, and oh, look, one by one, up close, into the face of each juror and give them my blessing:

Yes, my son, go on.

Scott said later, "I really like our jury."

"Yeah, me too," I said. And yet though I meant this, and so did Scott, I was troubled, and so was he. I saw the principal again. Why'd we pick *him?* Or did I mention that we had picked a hearing officer who decided unemployment cases? That is, we had picked as a juror . . . a man who was a *judge!* Isn't it true what every lawyer says, that to be a judge and see people beg for mercy every day dries up the guy, makes him mean and bitter?

"Yeah," said Scott. "We should have thought about him some more."

Yes, on our jury we had a judge: a small, nervous man in a windbreaker. I now sensed, He is an enemy, being a judge, etc., but *is* that really true? Maybe if litigants are always hitting on you, begging, etc., it lowers your defenses. In an interview, that's what the French actress Catherine Deneuve said about the men always hitting on her. She said the more they beg, etc.

But there's a difference between being a judge and being Catherine Deneuve, yes?

That's true, but there's other "evidence." A study just came out about awards of punitive damages, and it turns out that, on average, not juries but judges tend to give more "punies."

Oh?

That just proves judges are *less* compassionate, and more "punitive," that is, when a defendant is really out of line. No, I didn't trust the little guy in the windbreaker.

But then I forgot about him as more jurors came in.

"They're interested, at least," said Scott.

"Yeah, that's good." It's funny, how each juror seemed to wiggle in the chair in the same way and tried to say, "Oh, I'm not tainted!" Yes, I liked our jury.

Uh, a lot.

Only by nightfall, one could say, "Why, back then, didn't you guys move for a mistrial?" God knows, we saw some hard faces. Did I mention that we had picked a woman who had called the cops on her husband?

Anyway, the answer is, Judge K. would not have stopped it. All through he had been remarkable. For a moment, when the UIC kid came in, and he was wearing a "New York Yankees" T-shirt. . . . I saw Judge K. staring at that T-shirt, and I thought, He's going to lose it, but no, it was all: Would you like a cup of tea? No, Judge K. wanted this jury to stay put.

And the jury wanted to stay. I remember the last juror, a black woman. Also a schoolteacher. Her son was a journalist (bad sign). The Judge had started, "Now, with an impartial mind do you think you can hear this—?"

"OF COURSE!" she said, annoyed, and I thought, If she had a ruler, she would whack us.

But I really did like our jury. And I even liked the Judge, *and I even liked Ms. M.,* and maybe at this point I should take a moment to explain.

18. WHY I NOW LIKED MS. M.

First, because in this little room, a few inches from her, I really did feel now as if we were all a team.

Second, because she was smart, and could curse calm and off-hand, and not huff and puff and throw the ball like a girl.

Third, because there's a kind of "Gaia" effect at Twenty-sixth and Cal. The way "you" as the lawyer can become like the building, and the building can become a bit like "you." So maybe at first Ms. M.

seemed to be from another planet (and not Venus), but soon I, too, had the same little filmy thing, the biota of the building, creeping over me. Does that make sense?

But finally . . . and this is the big reason I came to like her . . . she was a prosecutor, and had the power. She won all the cases. In America prosecutors win all the time, and not just 90 or 95 percent, but all the time, in effect. And anyway, at this moment in our history, secretly don't we all want to prosecute? Oh, no, you say, I'm a liberal, or I'm a vegan, or even, I throw the ball like a girl, or *even,* I am a girl. And yet, I wonder if in our secret hearts, without knowing it, the idea of the prosecutor is shaping our very dreams. The French writers of long ago, like Rousseau and Montesquieu, used to bat around a theory: The *form* of a country's government stamps the *personality* or character of a people. What makes the French so "French"? The (Bourbon) monarchy. And the British so "British"? Parliament, and all the rest.

So what is shaping the personal secret lives of you and me if Rousseau is right? For us, I would think: the Special Prosecutor, who hovers with a subpoena over every native heart. Because of my childhood, I still fear that a leader (JFK), one who steps out, will be shot. But if I were a child now, wouldn't I fear that later if I step out, I will be prosecuted? Think of the limitless terror of many a child now, at age nine or ten, who thinks, If I step out, will I be zapped like President "Bill"? Now, I don't mean to pick on Starr, but only to cite him as a stand-in for all the prosecutors right now: Mr. S., Ms. M., more in number than at any time before. But who can blame the child who *wants* to be a prosecutor? In an age of inequality, when even lawyers are being stiffed in terms of pay (*most* lawyers), to be a prosecutor is really a way to even things up. "But the question," said a friend who's a teacher, "is whether prosecutors today are more abusive than before?" And later I had an answer: "One by one, maybe not. But the problem is, there are so many more!" Look, just since I left law school, the rate at which we imprison people has gone up *seven* times. (That's seven times more chances to do something wrong.) No, one by one, they may be "better," and maybe more went to Harvard and Yale, just as more people get prosecuted from Harvard and Yale, but it's no surprise, in a time of gridlock, that thousands try it for a while, three or four years, and we're breeding a generation of prosecutors, and exes, and wanna-bes, and everyone putting on airs.

And compared to these, Ms. M. was as smart, but she didn't put on airs. I didn't feel she might come after me, or Scott, or Judge K., the way I feel about many an assistant U.S. attorney. Judge K. was pro-state, of course, but he didn't seem to be in terror of her.

19. CHARTERHOUSE OF PARMA

Voir dire done, now Scott (and, uh, I) had to try the case! I was beat. I felt as I do when I've defended a five-hour dep, and go home, and lace my Sauconys, and stop. "I don't have an antioxidant left!" It would be bad to ask Scott, "Aren't you beat?" No. Don't. He'd told me that once as a P.D., he did little misdemeanors, like "loitering," and when he finished at one in the afternoon, "I'd go home just from that and sleep for two hours."

Now the jury came back as if nothing had happened, and Judge K. said, "I want to do this all before lunch."

WHAT? The whole trial, the two women, and then Rolando, and then do the closing statements? I thought, I'm too exhausted to sit in the chair, and closed my eyes.

When I opened them, Ms. M. was handing us sheets of paper, her "Proposed Jury Instructions." Each "instruction" was on a separate page. I looked at the first, its gist, more or less:

INSTRUCTION NO. I
LADIES AND GENTLEMEN, YOU ARE MEMBERS OF A JURY.

Or something equally childish. But to see a piece of paper with writing was a shock down here. I thought everyone danced naked around the fire. Scott handed me the Instruction on Compulsion. "Can you argue it?" Then he called the woman who was Rolando's boss at a flea market when Rolando was age ten. After her would be the girl from the bank, Rolando's fiancée.

Two brunettes. Two very pretty Latina women. Right after Calvin. What could they say about the murder?

Nothing.

But this was Scott's brilliance. Somehow, get them up there, dark, lovely, a moment of mantilla, though both of them were business or accounting majors. The excuse for calling each woman was to testify as to Rolando's "character."

As to "character," the rules in evidence are nutty. You can't testify as to what you personally know, say, about Rolando's goodness. For example: "I know he was a good kid because he was good to my little dog." You can't say that. Rather you can testify only as to what you heard *other people* other than yourself say. For example: "I heard *other people* say how he was good to little dogs."

Nutty? Yes, but the point was somehow to get the two young women up there.

The first woman, his boss, pretty, seemed like she was no more than thirty. What she tried to say was: Rolando was the kind of boy who tried to "please." Make the adults happy.

This fit Scott's case: to please, he was a kid who changed a *taht* to *that*.

But the rules of evidence are so nutty it was hard even to set her up to say this. Scott would say, for example, "Ms. ———, what was Rolando like as an employee?"

Objection.

Sustained.

"When did he start work—?"

Objection, etc. After Mr. S. popped up three times, I wanted to choke him. But of course that's not allowed.

Evidence in law school is for babies. Yet what amazes me is how even the oldest of the pros stumble over little rules. Even in this case, I recall Mr. S. objecting once and the Judge sustaining, and Scott asking for a side bar, and even though he had sustained, the Judge now asked Mr. S.:

"Basis?"

"Relevancy."

"Oh," said the Judge. "I sustained for hearsay."

I started to laugh, but stopped in time. On the way back, I said to Scott, "I thought hearsay was all right."

It was for reputation. For the testimony of the two brunettes.

One business major down, Scott called the next. The whole point was to get the girl to say, "I'm Rolando's fiancée."

As she walked up, I thought, I'm one of the few who knows she's Rolando's fiancée. If I'd been irked at her reading legal thrillers, now I felt shaky. My eyes were moist. I thought again, If he went in at fifteen . . . how could this girl, smart, so pretty, be his fiancée?

Scott said, "What is your relation to the defendant?"

"I'm his fiancée." She did not look at the jury. (What did they think?)

"And how long," said Scott, "have you known him?"

"Since he was eleven."

The Judge, as if he had to write something, now put his head down. A few of the jurors seemed to be . . . chewing.

On the other hand, Mr. S. was not objecting. How could he? These were just preliminaries.

But I kept thinking, as Scott had said, "It says a lot about Rolando that he has a fiancée."

Was it so strange? In *La Vita Nuovo,* Dante's first poem, he fell in love with Beatrice when she was nine. But the poem is a little strange. The young poet sees in a dream a young girl, like Beatrice . . . naked, on a crimson cloth, and a Mysterious Figure wakes the girl, and gives her a glowing object, the poet's heart, *which she begins to eat!* I'll put the book down.

My point being, just because this could also have happened to Dante doesn't mean it isn't strange.

What was strange about the testimony was that Scott could ask only about Rolando's reputation.

"Did you," he said, "know people who knew Rolando?"

"Y-yes."

She seemed to be eating her heart.

"And," Scott said, "did you form an impression as to his reputation . . . for integrity?" Scott could ask about each "virtue."

"Y-yes." Her voice broke.

"And what . . . what was his reputation?"

She tried to speak normally. "It was . . . Oh! It was an excellent reputation!"

I took a gulp of air. Oh, Scott, stop! It was heartbreaking, but he asked, "And did you form an impression, etc., etc . . . for his honesty?"

That moment what a look she gave Scott! What was I doing, sitting next to Rolando?

"It . . ." She was going to answer, "It was . . . an excellent reputation!"

I whispered to myself, Stop, Scott, please! I glanced at the jury. Two or three of them were . . . chewing.

I expected Ms. M. would cross-examine. Or just waive it. But no, Mr. S. was getting up, and went right up in her face. "So," he snapped at her. "You tell us of your opinion as to his Reputation-in-the-Community. Tell us . . ."

He turned to the jury.

" . . . when was the last time you *talked* to anyone about his Reputation-in-the-Community?" Of course he had set a trap. Rolando had been locked up for seven years. But if she said, "Seven years ago," her testimony would be destroyed.

" . . . When was the last time you—?"

She stared at Mr. S.: "Six months ago. With Jill Garcia."

And she looked right at him.

Oh, Mr. S.! Sit down, buddy. And now Scott called up Rolando.

20. ROLANDO'S TURN

After the jury's verdict I went to St. Al's for Good Friday. After the Gospel, the Spanish-speaking Catholics go downstairs to a chapel, underground, for "their" homily, while our priest upstairs continues in English. "Why," said "our" priest, "is the Passion on Good Friday always from John?" Because, he explained, John's is the one Gospel in which Jesus is in control. "This is important because in the Latin countries, such as Mexico, Good Friday has a way of overshadowing Easter." As it may for those who went downstairs (he did not say this). To counter this, the Church has us read only from John, where Jesus is not a fugitive, hunted and scared, but Jesus is a King, regal and in control. In the other Gospels, Jesus is someone whose back is against the wall. And the Gospel of John, said the priest, was also, for the early Christians, a way of preparing them for court! Here I woke up. Yes, said the priest, it is a model of how a Christian answers at a trial. Be like Jesus with Pilate. Be strong and in control.

•   •   •

So at this trial. It was a way to see the two "directs."

Calvin, in control, or upright as in John. Rolando, his back against the wall.

His turn now.

As he rose to testify, I tried, but couldn't, get my hand up there on his shoulder. I looked at Judge K. Why couldn't he let us break for lunch? But the Judge wanted to finish. "Do you swear, etc.?"

As Rolando took the oath, I thought, Oh, he wants to run! As I would have. It's one thing to be the Jesus in John's Gospel and in control. But that Jesus had a destiny. What if you aren't supposed to have a destiny, and prison, the loss of your own life, it's just a mistake. It's odd how in 100, 200 A.D. Christian martyrs line up, smiling, to die. Jesus in the other Gospels wants to live!

Notes on Rolando as a witness: Didn't use "quotes" like Calvin. Nervous on direct. Still, Scott was able to get him through it.

An example:

"And then, you say, you met this older boy. What was his name?"

"I don't know," Rolando said. "It was just a guy."

See? Not as good as Calvin. Scott went on: "What did he tell you?"

"I did what . . . what they asked me to."

Or another time, he said, "I . . . I was scared that if I ran away, they would do . . . something."

Something?

It's a pedantic point, but this is what I mean about Calvin being a better witness. Calvin would have quoted, word for word. On my yellow pad I scrawled, "SAY, 'THEY WERE GOING TO HURT MY FAMILY!!!' "

Ah! No way to get a note to him.

From far back I thought again how in the dark of state prison Rolando had seemed to grow up bent or crooked, as if in such a place

his DNA had been bleating: "We don't want to pop out inside here!"
Anyway, as he hunched over, Scott took him through the night.

Back of the bar.

Empty lot.

The threat.

Calvin had said, "I took out a gun . . ." Ah! Rolando forgot to
mention the gun!

Now I was afraid as Mr. S. stood to cross. (When were we having
lunch?) Because Mr. S. had planned his cross to tear apart our case that
the boy had been "compelled." He wanted to show that at each point
that night Rolando had had a chance to run.

Or, legally speaking: a Reasonable Man's chance to run. Remember, this is an adult court. Even if you're a boy, you have to be the Reasonable Man.

Mr. S. was small. But on cross, he seemed to tower over poor
Rolando, who was sitting hunched up in a Big Bird type of way.

Mr. S.: At the bar, you were at the front?

R: Yes.

Mr. S.: You and Tim at the back.

R: Y-yes.

Mr. S.: So there was nothing between you and the front door. You
could have run!

R: They . . . had guns.

Mr. S.: You could have *run!* Did they have a gun to your head?

R: I . . . No.

(I thought, Good, Rolando, let him have a point.)

Mr. S.: *No!* That's right! There wasn't any gun! And on the street
. . . you could have run!

R: I . . . was scared!

Mr. S.: Didn't you agree to meet up with Tim and Calvin, after
the holdup?

R: I was . . .

Mr. S.: You seemed to know where to go, *didn't you?*

What I put down is not a "transcript," but I have tried to write it down as I recall. For I was taking notes now, fearful, as if this whole nightmare might be gone later on, just a dream. Especially the way Rolando kept saying, "I was scared."

Mr. S.: Scared? At the station didn't you say that Tim and Calvin did it? At the station you weren't "scared." Here's your confession. Why didn't you say, "They forced me"?

R: I . . . don't know . . .

Mr. S.: Let me read your confession—

And it's true, at the station, Rolando had not said that Tim and Calvin forced him. I can explain, I think. At the station, Rolando would not have wanted to accuse Calvin, who was still at large, of a second crime, a kidnapping: a crime against Rolando *himself.* That was Scott's theory. At the station, as on the night of the murder, he was just a kid who wanted to run away.

Maybe, too, on the stand, he was reliving it, and had become one last time . . . just a kid. Who wanted to run away! Mr. S., running after him, chasing him down every alley.

As a lawyer, I felt helpless. Scott could object if Mr. S. cut off an answer, but Mr. S. was careful not to do that.

By the way, why wasn't *Ms. M.* doing this cross? In the first trial she had done the cross. But Mr. S. did it, I believe, for two reasons: (1) The way Scott had reworked the case, with compulsion as the issue, she couldn't do the same cross she had a few years ago, and (2) Rolando, this time, was not a boy but a man. So Mr. S. would be the cop. Or maybe since she had done Calvin, it was Mr. S.'s turn.

At any rate he was good, the way he chased him.

Mr. S.: Out on the street, you could have run?

R: I was scared.

Three little words: *I. Was. Scared.* He used his mantra like a little bat, fouling off the pitches of a Machine.

He was scared, I was scared. So scared that he forgot to say that Calvin took out a gun and made him take the money! Finally, it was over. Mr. S. sat down. Scott leaned over: "I think Rolando did pretty well and I'm not going to redirect. You agree?"

Yes, of course! But having no sense, I whispered back, "Why don't we bring out how Rolando couldn't *accuse* Calvin of kidnapping, you know, be his accuser?" Scott frowned. So I wrote out on my pad:

"Let's ask, YOU DIDN'T WANT TO BRING CHARGES FOR WHAT THEY DID TO *YOU?*" I handed it over, and Scott frowned even more. "I can't ask a question like that," he whispered.

"Why not?"

"He wouldn't understand it!"

"Oh."

"Your Honor," said Scott in a loud voice, "no further questions." If we had asked any, Mr. S. would have had the right to recross and rip into him even more. And the main thing was to get Rolando out of there.

As Rolando sat next to me, I gave him a little smile: Way to Go. But I was shivering the way he'd kept saying I Was Scared.

21. MOOT COURT

"Okay, ladies and gentlemen," said Judge K. to the jury. "We're going to excuse you. The lawyers have some chores to attend to. Then we'll bring you back in here for closing argument." As they went out, it was All Rise. We rise, I read somewhere, because a jury is a body of twelve, as in the Twelve Apostles.

"So," I said to Scott, "*now* do we get our lunch?" But I had to argue an Instruction: the *big* one on Compulsion.

In fact now that the trial was over, I *wanted* to argue. After all, Scott had done everything! I was ashamed. Look, I thought, how Ms. M. and Mr. S. had worked together. Oh, I'd helped, in a third-mate kind of way. How? Handing things to Scott.

I could have done a witness, but I hate to ask questions. True, I do a lot of civil depositions, but they take place offstage, with no one watching. Even those I dread. Except that when I actually do start a dep, I often swing the other way. That's when I have no fear. I bore in. Sometimes I lock my eyes on the one I am deposing until I make the person look away, or even cry out, "I DID IT." Or: "I BURIED PAUL."

What pleasure to hear that! Even if it's only from a court reporter when I ask her, "Will you label this exhibit?"

Now I got my notes together. Nothing serious was about to happen, except that I'd make my first and only appearance in this court! So perhaps now is the time to say why, as a lawyer, I *really* went to law school in the first place. It was not because I was the "oldest child," or wanted to be a Big Firm Partner, and least of all, to avenge myself on the Puritans. No, at a moment like this, I know the real reason I went. It was simple:

I wanted to toughen up.

I'd become soft as a sixties undergrad. After each spring they'd cancel all exams, etc. Now, in the nineteenth century at Harvard College, many a young man decided, as I did, I have to toughen up. Some went off to sea, like Richard Henry Dana in *Two Years Before the Mast*. Some went out West, like Francis Parkmam, who took on *The Oregon Trail*.

But by the time I was in college, there was a new and better way for a kid like me to "toughen up." That was . . . just go to the law school across the street. So all I did was cross the street. And the first day in Property, I thought, This isn't going to work. We had to read a stupid case about a fox. If the fox were "in the wild," and no one owned it, how did anyone get to own a fox, or something.

Any hands, class?

I figured no one would bother with so dumb a question. But it was like a gun went off, and a hundred kids began to howl. Soon to my horror, we were all on our horses, and riding, and shouting, "Who's got the fox?"

And right off, kids were slashing each other with whips. I was appalled. Was it going to be like this for three more years? How odd, I now think, that other guys our age were killing in Vietnam. For the new unequal America, law school may have been the better way to toughen up.

Then came our First Year Moot Court. I was to argue an instruction . . . indeed, it was about compulsion. In Rolando's case "my" issue was: Did he or did the State have to prove he was "coerced"? Which party had the Burden, as we like to say?

In my Moot Court twenty-five years ago, I had a similar issue to argue. This time I was playing "the state," and it was a rape case in which the woman did not struggle. So the issue in that far-off time was: Did the state have to prove that this act of intercourse was "against her will," subjectively, or only "without her consent," objectively?

To frame the "compulsion" issue, did the state have to prove the victim was compelled, or did the alleged rapist have to prove she was *not* compelled?

I was trying to remember what I'd said, back as a law student, as I prepared as an adult to argue for Rolando now.

Ah, I couldn't remember. All I could remember was that my opponent, Jo, was the Smartest in Our Class. Literally, at the end, he had the highest grade. Maybe ever. That's who, by lot, I was up against. For weeks I thought, I'm going to be destroyed!

I thought this because each week I had to revise my "brief" and give it to our Moot Court Coach. And each week, our Moot Court Coach would glance at my brief, shake his head and moan:

"God, you should see *Jo's brief!*"

So I knew he was going to destroy me. But then I ran into my First Year Advisor, and I told him I was going to be destroyed. "No," he laughed. "You're not going to be destroyed." So what if Jo is the Smartest? Doesn't matter in the real world.

Really?

Then, as an example, he named my Contracts teacher, Professor B. "You won't believe this, but already, at your age, you could go into court, and you could 'take' Professor B.!" And his reason was, or so I recall, that a court is the opposite of law school class, where everyone shouted "GET THE FOX!" In a class, a Contracts teacher like Professor B. could jump, foxlike, from one little point to the other, and I had no time to think, or keep up. But in Moot Court there was . . . well, one little issue, right?

One issue: Did the state have to show sex was compelled?

But instead of two seconds, I had two *months,* in which to crawl, slowly, up to the level where Jo would be in two seconds in a class. Hare and Tortoise. He'd been at the finish line for weeks, but slowly I would get there. Same with my teacher, B.

You can take B.! That's what my Advisor said.

Yes, come on, toughen up. I kept thinking, Yes, I can take B.!

But it was silly, I didn't want to "take" B. at all. Even in Moot Court, I secretly yearned for a way to settle. But that was out, and anyway my Advisor kept saying, "YOU CAN TAKE B.," and I was lacing up my gloves.

Maybe it was true, I CAN TAKE B.!

But I was up against Jo, and he of course destroyed me.

. . .

The big issue in my Moot Court had been: Do we apply the Objective or Subjective Standard? Your Honor, we know the rape was without her consent (external). We cannot know if it was against her will (internal, subjective). The point of Schopenhauer's whole philosophy is that we aren't able to know the subjective, i.e., the "will," as we can know an external concept, e.g., "the idea" of consent. That's why he called his book *The World as Will and Idea*.

I'm kidding, I didn't literally cite Schopenhauer in Moot Court.

But how can we know, ever know, what Rolando felt *inside?* He was scared! It was *Subjective.*

But Mr. S. wanted to add a new and special instruction. "The defense of compulsion is not available if the defendant had an opportunity to flee."

He could Run! It was all *Objective.*

Our side hated this instruction. Of course he had a chance to *flee.* But it's not so smart to argue the merits, is it? They're the State. We're the Little Guy.

Ah, but I had a much better, last-ditch argument to make. Your Honor, Mr. S. is offering a *new* instruction—it is *not* one of the Instructions in the Big Brown Book we photocopy out of! Judge, it's not in the Brown Book!

Oh, after this, I went into a riff about the Objective v. the Subjective Standard, and Who Has the Burden, until everyone had a headache. Ms. M., Scott, Mr. S., they all did. But that part about Schopenhauer-type stuff was just my Victory Lap. My main point was: Where is it in the Big Brown Book?

Whether Judge K. decided on that basis I will never know. Judge K., too, seemed to have a mild headache. At any rate, he frowned at the State's new instruction and said, "Well . . . at this time . . . I . . . I'm not going to give the instruction." (We win!) But then with another frown, at us: "But that's just for the time being. If the jury asks for clarification later, I'll probably give this, understand?"

"Yes, Your Honor!" I curtsied in the Eddie Haskell way that civil lawyers do, and he probably didn't care for it.

Now could we go to lunch?

22. WHAT SCOTT TOLD THE JURY

No, we couldn't. Though it was now after one P.M., the Judge said, "Let's go to the closing statements."

To Scott, who looked beat, I said, "You tired?"

He grinned. "Sure! But what can I do?"

Maybe my own headache may have come from not eating. The jury came back. I felt sorry for Ms. M., since she had to speak first.

But Mr. S. stood up to speak. Why? Maybe Ms. M. had the worse headache. I even felt sorry for Mr. S. as he struggled through his closing. (No, I didn't.) Over and over he said:

"He could have run! He could have run!"

I was sighing very loud. Mr. S., I'd like to see you run. His closing was a rehash of his cross of Rolando. No surprise, since his cross had taken place only a few minutes before. So if this trial were like a ball game, he'd be like an announcer still marveling at the last play.

Now Scott rose for our closing. The day before I had asked what he'd say. "Don't you get up there and argue how hard it is to show 'Beyond Reasonable Doubt'?"

He shook his head. "They tell you not to do that in Trial School."

Really? I thought that's what all defense lawyers did. Out in Pittsburgh a guy told me, "I have about three quarters of my closing in the can. All I do is talk to them, the jury, about *Beyond Reasonable Doubt*. I talk about *each* word. I keep going . . . forty, forty-five minutes . . .

until I see them nodding, and then when they really got it . . . then, finally, I get to the facts."

I thought, Hey, that must be right. He said he'd had eight acquittals. Eight of them in a row!

But then, Scott may be right. When I was flipping through the Brown Book, I saw one instruction that said, " 'Beyond reasonable doubt' does not mean beyond *reasonable* doubt." Because it's "reasonable" to have, well, some doubt.

Yes, that's clear.

But is it clear? Because then I saw an instruction that said, no it's not reasonable to have some doubt. So anyway I could see why they tell you at Trial School, "Stay *away* from that!"

Later I wondered, if I'd been let up to argue, what would I have said?

"Ladies and gentlemen . . . I don't know whether it's reasonable to have doubt or reasonable not to have doubt. People can argue this either way.

"But what's not reasonable is putting away a kid, who's fifteen, for forty years.

"And speaking of reasonable, what's reasonable about the Senate not ratifying the International Convention? If we ratified that treaty, we wouldn't even have to be here."

That's the closing I'd like to give. And if I did, it would be the Closing of My Law Career. If I said that, I'd be disbarred. It's strange that while I could say this on a street corner, I can't say it in a court, because in a court the First Amendment doesn't apply. I'm in a police state.

Despite the First Amendment, I can't ask a jury to consider the law. How the conservatives love to scream that America faces a crisis: jury nullification. Juries failing to follow the law. Look at O.J., etc.

To all the guff about juries ignoring the law, I'd like to point out two little facts:

1. Since I got out of law school, the rate of imprisoning people has risen not two, not three, not four . . . but *seven* times. If a jury were using *any* version of Beyond Reasonable Doubt, it is hard to see how the rate of imprisoning people could shoot up seven times above historic levels. But whether that's the case or not, we at least know this: jury nullification can hardly be a problem if the rate of imprisoning people has shot up seven times.

2. The right should be in favor of jury nullification. Or at least the Federalist Society should be. This is the right-wing group that started out promoting the views of Federalists such as James Madison, John Jay, based on not much more than that all of them wore powdered wigs. Then somebody in the Federalist Society began to *read* the Federalists, who in fact believed in a central government. "My God, we're not in favor of this." So they switched over and became Anti-Federalists.

But the problem with switching over to the Anti-Federalists is that Patrick Henry and his friends liked jury nullification, too. Yes, let the jury toss out the drug laws, etc.

Okay, so they could switch back now to the Federalists, but John Jay, et al., believed in jury nullification, too. As Chief Justice, John Jay drafted a famous jury instruction that in America a jury has the right *to determine the law!*

So there is precedent if a lawyer like me wants to tell the jury they should look to international law, since this must be, in the end, consistent with our Constitution. Let the jury decide! I could cite every one of the Founders in my defense. And after that, I'd be disbarred.

Yet why not let our juries stop trying kids as adults or criminalizing drugs? My brother was just on a jury in a drug case. "We voted to convict," he said. "It's like our foreman said, there isn't any doubt the guy did it. But for me—I'm telling you it's the last time."

"Why?" I said.

"Why should I as a taxpayer pay twenty thousand dollars a year to keep a guy like this in jail?"

And if lawyers like Scott could argue this, the rate of imprisoning people wouldn't go up seven times. But no one has the nerve to start the nullifying.

We're not allowed, even though the Founders said we were. When did this change? The judges in this country aren't that naive. They figure out a way to say: It's always been this way, etc.

But here's a chilling thought: That the reason this has all happened, i.e., the whopping increase in the prison rate, the decline of any jury resistance, etc., is that people are getting stupider. Now, at first this seems like me being, still, alas, a bit sophomoric. (A bit?) But I've been haunted by something my friend Cece said the other night. We were dining at a place called Café Matou, which is a bistro-type place in what used to be a hard-core blue-collar block near Nelson Algren's house. Now it's bistro land, with a lot of blondes bubbling in the standard upscale way. Cece was half listening to a table of them (I heard nothing) and then leaned over and said:

"Don't you think people are getting stupider?"

NO! I said. Because I'm too far out there on the Left now. But I was louder than I should have been, because of course I think they are. But I said:

"How can you say that? Cece, you don't know about those people."

She sighed. "Forty years ago, those girls over there would have been sitting at a local coffee shop. At the counter. The kind of place I knew growing up. You know?"

She paused.

"Maybe they said the same things back then. Maybe these things just sound stupider in Café Matou."

But there's a study in the *Harvard Law Review* that jurors can't comprehend or understand the instructions. And let's not blame the public schools. Unlike forty or fifty years ago, many more of these jurors have been to college.

Maybe it's because so many people have gone to college that people have gotten stupider. But consider all the ways or measures by which people have gotten stupider:

Newspapers? Copy shrinking. Mimics TV.

Literacy? In decline.

Books? Mid-list books are nearly extinct.

Movies? Ha.

Voting? Falling under 50 percent.

All this at a time when education is shooting up. Pick up a big-city newspaper of a Midwest town from sixty years ago. Even the evening paper in Cincinnati of sixty years ago . . . by our standards now, it reads like *The New York Times.*

But scariest of all . . . what about me? I compare myself to my forebears, who lived in a time when people, even high school grads, wrote in long, mellifluous sentences that had weight and balance and parallel structure, and in my own case it's a struggle to get out a sentence as complicated or lengthy as: "Are people getting stupider?"

Anyway, Scott walked up now to give his closing.

23. THE SMARTEST THING

What used to drive me nuts about Clinton, on TV in a debate, is that he'd be so "soft," and I'd be thinking, "Come on, there's Dole, why don't you hit back? But of course that's how he *did* "hit back."

By being "soft." So the point is, to be like Bill. Be "soft," in the TV sense.

Scott was soft that way. He didn't froth as I would have, and his closing was a model of how—you—talk—to—juries—now. If only they'd been at home and watching on TV, the rest would have been as simple as another Clinton term.

Alas, there would be things Scott could not control.

Anyway, he was perfect. He spoke with the calm of a dad who does Little League. "Remember what it was like when we were kids, and other kids came around to say, 'Let's take this kid's bat. . . . ,' or 'Let's swipe his ball. . . . '? Well, Rolando lived in a place where kids were not like that. The ones who came up and threatened him? They were going to rob a bar. . . ."

He paused. "And he was just a kid!

"He was just a kid in the wrong place." He looked at them as if they were his neighbors.

"And of course he didn't 'go to the police' after it was over. You remember the feeling when you were a kid and something bad happened? Really bad?"

He paused.

"You shut your eyes. You think, as a kid, If I shut my eyes, maybe it'll go away."

A woman juror looked over.

"That's what Rolando did. After this was over, he didn't want to think about this, ever again. Like a nightmare.

"He just wanted it to go away."

I wondered if Rolando knew how hard it is, for a lawyer like Scott, to make this seem so easy! If I'd done it, I'd have started blithering about . . . oh, the Convention on the Child. What a mess I'd have made.

As Scott neared the end, I had a sense that, right next to me, something was going wrong. When I turned . . .

Ah! Rolando was staring, in a scary way, at the jury! What, do I tell him not to stare? I now saw that at least two of the jurors were staring back.

I was so rattled, I missed Scott's final line. Then I saw him picking up his papers and turning to walk back.

When he sat, he said, in a whisper, "How was it?"

I was still so rattled. "Good." It's all I said.

Then I remembered he was a lawyer, and to some extent he was performing. So I was about to say more, like: "No, you were great!" And it was over! Then—a horrible thing happened.

Ms. M. *stood!* She began walking toward the jury, and shouting: ". . . yes, and what of James Lyons! What of the man who died!"

"What the . . . what is she doing?" I said under my breath.

"Oh," said Scott, "this is the part I hate." That in a criminal case, the state has a *rebuttal!* In effect, two closing arguments. Until Ms. M. went up there, I'd had no idea that both Ms. M. *and* Mr. S. would argue to the jury.

Now I knew why the state does convict everybody. The state goes first. The state then ends. The defense just gets to mumble in the middle.

And Ms. M., to finish, was really shouting. "YES, THE DECEASED JAMES LYONS WOULD BE ALIVE TODAY. . . . AND HE WILL NEVER SEE A SUNRISE. . . . BUT DOES THIS DEFENDANT EVEN CARE? . . ."

I'd have sighed like Al Gore, but no one would have heard me. Scott said, "Put your hand on Rolando, you have to show you're with him."

But he didn't say where to put my hand. What part of Rolando? But now Ms. M. had walked over to our table to point at the poor boy, and at that instant . . .

I put my hand on him. Bam. Very natural.

Anyway, she went on shouting, though she didn't seem that mad at him.

Now, when Ms. M. finished, I thought, At last I can have lunch! But Judge K. had begun to read the instructions. Maybe he was hungry, too, because when he started off reading, "Instruction Number One . . . ," they began to whizz by like boxcars.

The instruction on compulsion, which I had sweated over? Whoosh. I never heard it. Oh well, he'll give them copies. I forgot, since I never do a jury trial.

Anyway the jury rose, and we stood to show "respect." Some of these people had come in from the suburbs.

And now I said to Scott, "Let's eat!"

24. LET'S EAT!

But the cafeteria was closed. What's left, Gangbangers Lounge?

"No," said Scott. "We can walk up to Twenty-sixth Street and get a pizza."

"Up there?" Up on Twenty-sixth, I thought everything was Mexican. It's called Little Village. Besides, it's a hike. "What if the jury comes back?" I said.

"I've got a beeper," said Scott.

Though it was 2:45 P.M, it was dark out. Was this wise? I'd been so happy ("Let's eat!"), and now I was depressed.

"It's so far," I said.

As we walked up to Twenty-sixth, I saw a kid who was Latino and thin and fifteen or so, then another, and each kid made me think, Why is he out here, and Rolando's not? And it was odd, and I was scared for them.

It was depressing anyway to be in Little Village. It made me think of a night long ago when I came down here on a date with L., and with her, I'd do the damndest things to be romantic. This one really was. It was the night before Easter, or Holy Saturday. We walked past churches with doors open, and in the naves in the dark kids were lighting candles. And walking like the people of Israel, through a dry path in the sea. And if not romantic, at least it was all terribly Spanish. And was it that night . . . or it must have been another night, when she put the rose up in her hair. Yes, it was also at a Latin club, right before Easter (again). As I parked the car, I handed L. a rose. "What do I do with this?" she said. Oh, I said, you put it in your hair. And I meant it as a joke, but when she did so, it was anything but a joke. And I had a shock. To braid it, she had to pull down her visor, the one on the "woman's side," and I found out that my car had a little mirror with white lights. Like a mirror on a woman's dressing table. How odd to find that my Ford Escort, where I stuffed my gym bag, all along had secretly had in it—a *boudoir.*

Oh, to have that night back now!

"Here's a Popeye's," Scott said, "but let's go up here to this place. It's Italian."

Yeah. It was "Italian."

When I opened the door, I had to look *down.* It was like opening a door into a storm cellar. And while it's true I could smell a pizza . . . I could hear a broken toilet, and water sloshing. Back in what may have been a "kitchen," there was a pool of something slopping over rotted wood. The sound of the slop–slop was so loud, it almost drowned out the TV, but didn't.

A group of lawyers (public defenders?) were drinking pretty heavily at a bar. It also seemed the safest thing to do. Our waitress came over. She gave me a glass of . . . "water."

"Ready to order, guys?"

Scott ordered a pizza. I wasn't hungry. "You have any tuna?" I said. These P.D.s were really drinking. Of course, I guess I'd be drinking too if in every one of my cases the state had two closings.

Exhausted, Scott shut his eyes. Then from another table, a woman shouted,

"SCOTT!"

She waved, and came over. She was a Public Defender too, and an old friend of Scott's, and behind her I saw a girl, maybe in her early twenties. She turned out to be a law student, helping Scott's friend.

Scott and the P.D. began to talk, and I kept staring at the "student." Something was *wrong* with this kid, and not the fact she was twenty years younger than anyone else. It was the way she was . . . smiling. Happy. Really happy.

And rocking, on her toes.

Had she been drinking? I looked at the guys at the bar. There was a man, eyes rolling, with hair plastered and parted in the middle, like Alfalfa or somebody in *Spanky and Our Gang*.

No, she couldn't have been at the bar. Could she?

But the way she was rocking on her toes! Anyway, the woman P.D. began to talk to Scott and me.

"The pizza here is okay," she said.

"Yeah," said Scott. "It's okay."

"Yeah, it's sort of okay," she said. Then she looked at me: "So? Why aren't you drinking?"

"It's only three o'clock."

"Oh, come on!" she laughed. "You just did a TRIAL!"

"I didn't really."

"What's the point of trying a CASE," she said, "if you aren't going to DRINK?"

"I . . . I don't know," I said. And I didn't either. The law student was still rocking on her toes.

Then the P.D. smiled, and said, to lift my spirits, "There are lots of stories how lawyers—and judges—come over here to drink when the jury is 'out,' at night. Yeah, judges too! And they get beeped that the jury is coming out, and they go back, the jury comes out and the lawyers, they try to stand . . . but they *can't,* because everyone's BOMBED!"

The girl, the student, was laughing. I wanted to say, "Hmpf! We don't do this in 'Civil,' young lady!" But I doubt she'd have stopped laughing.

It's good, I suppose, for the kids to get a taste of Real Law; i.e. to engage in blind drinking in storm cellars as they look up at daytime TV.

The P.D. was doing a murder case. "Right now," she said to Scott, "we're about to head up to Rogers Park, to interview a witness."

Oh, Rogers Park. I nodded. I used to live there. A friend calls it "Mayberry with a crime problem." A very big one.

The girl was rocking on her toes. Later I would talk to a lawyer who supervises law students like her in a clinic for criminal law. "Yeah," he said, "it's something, isn't it? You should see them by third year, the way they talk: 'Oh yeah, is that the girl who had the sex with her old man and then he shot her, or is she the one whose mother choked her with a cord?' It's sad, you know, the loss of their . . . innocence."

I was thinking of mine.

And yet the funny thing was, when I was in law school, I was like that girl rocking on her toes. Only back then what excited me was . . . basically, the Warren Court. I would have gone into any storm cellar to meet a Justice Black.

Anyway, I finished up my tuna, and we went up to get some air.

25. A DULL PATCH, IN THE LIBRARY

Scott's beeper was not beeping. When would this jury acquit? I kept saying to Scott, "If they did software for this stuff, it would have to kick out A-C-Q-U-I-T." Calvin said he pulled a gun, the State didn't rebut!

I kept saying this, but still the beeper didn't beep. We had to walk somewhere. Why not the library?

"That's an idea," said Scott.

It was empty but for one black man all alone at the circulation desk. "Hello! Gentlemen! Will you sign in?" He kept saying:

"Will you sign in?"

He was nice, but he was weird. What, is this a motel? Okay. I looked for a pen. As I wrote, I could see that no one had signed in here for . . . hmm . . . weeks? Months?

"No one comes here much, huh?" I said. By this I meant that with the Westlaw, Lexis search engines, no one uses law libraries now. Whatever I said, it made him stare, twitch in a weird way. What *did* I say?

"Please, gentlemen, sign here. . . . ," he was pleading.

Okay, I'm signing.

Now, it was as if I'd pulled a sword from the stone. The light changed. He began to smile. A big smile. "Gentlemen," he said, "gentlemen . . . I have to go!"

He said again, "I have to . . . leave! It's three thirty . . . time to close . . . but don't worry, no, you can stay . . . please . . . gentlemen, you can stay!"

He'd show us how to lock up, and he did. And then . . . poof, he was gone. And it hit me for the first time that maybe we were prisoners. "Well," I said to Scott, "it seems as if we're in charge."

•   •   •

Scott nodded, and went off to read the *Law Bulletin*. I was wondering, Why doesn't the beeper go off? Scott was reading now. What else could he do? I tried to do a time sheet. Only one entry: "Rolando . . . 9.0," as in nine hours of billable time, though who am I going to bill?

"Maybe I should go back to the office."

"I have to stay," said Scott. "If I go back there and the beeper goes off, it'd take me half an hour to get down here." He paused. "Anyway, I can't concentrate if I'm waiting for a jury."

I looked around. Well . . . maybe I could look up a case? Once, in law libraries I used to come up here and read treatises. Williston. Corbin. I bet the girl, rocking on her toes, doesn't do that.

No, it's a different time. My God, at her age, I wouldn't have dreamed of doing criminal law, or think that one day I'd even be for a minute at Twenty-sixth and Cal. Once, when I was twenty-two, all I wanted to do was read the *Harvard Law Review,* which I used to flip through, like a magazine, say, *The New Republic* or *The Nation,* just for its politics.

O, Law Library of my youth!

Bill and Hillary Clinton, back in my day, first met in a law library. And while the two of them were making study dates and falling in love, I was in the library too. Sitting by myself, of course, and nibbling on my oatmeal cookies, and spilling the crumbs all over the articles in the law reviews.

Oh, how I loved the reviews, and I'd wait for the next issues. Back then some were like magazines, and they were covering, to me, the biggest story of them all:

How America, day by day, seemed to hurtle to equality.

Case after case on Equal Protection. Year by year the nature of it seemed to change. First there was Equal Protection: Race. Then came Equal Protection: Right to Travel, Vote, etc. But just ahead, any day now, there would be Equal Protection: Wealth. Cases on school financing, on welfare.

That was the running story that I was following, up in the library, with my cookies. I used to come back from a swim, and as the chlorine wafted off my skin, how happy I was to doze, and wake, and doze, and as I would read in my waking moments about the Warren Court, it seemed I was becoming an even more virtuous citizen.

I really thought we were coming to a reign of virtue. Montesquieu the French philosopher, has an uncanny definition of what "civic virtue" is: "Love of homeland, that is, love of equality."

Now, I didn't support, and still don't, my homeland in a war like Vietnam, but at least I loved equality. I didn't see, at the time, that we had to keep loving both.

I just wanted, I expected, more and more equality. I couldn't see back then that labor unions would collapse and that inequality would grow. Even if I had, I'd have had no sense then of what inequality alone would lead to:

more capital punishment
bigger prisons
"three strike" life sentences
kids growing up in jails

I couldn't see this, at twenty-two, that there could be a flip side to Montesquieu. That there could be a love of inequality. And it could grow, like a fire in our brains.

Two British criminologists in a study I saw in *Scientific American,* show by graph how a country's prison rate is tied to the coefficient of income inequality. That explains the paradox: How can a country as rich as ours have a prison rate that has shot past Russia's?

The two authors show that if you know the coefficient of inequality, you can crank out, in a formulalike way, how many will be in prison. Well . . . more or less.

I should have been reading *Scientific American*. Anyway, who saw this coming? Remember, I was educated to be a lawyer in what was going to be a "European-type" social democracy. So now, at Twenty-sixth and Cal, I look like a guy in spats. How absurd I must seem. Three years of law school, which cost my parents a fortune, twenty years of practice, and not once could I get anyone out of jail!

But no one told me it would be like this. Even in this trial, I talk about Rolando's age, fifteen, in the way that I thought about the age "fifteen" when I was in law school. Back then, "fifteen" meant you weren't dangerous, the way you were at "twenty-two." But now if you look at the statistics, "twenty-two" is the age when you are less likely to kill. So if I went in front of a jury and said, "He's only fifteen," a jury of today, unlike a jury when I was young, would be rational in concluding, "That must prove he did it."

It's sad that no one is in these libraries now. Imagine, today, Bill and Hillary would never have met. They'd be in their dorms with their computers.

I felt very sad, my youth is over. Oh, if I could have it back . . . I'd try to be like that girl, rocking on her toes. Anyway, Scott had folded up his paper now and came over and said, "Let's go back and see Rolando."

26. A TABLE AT CHARLIE TROTTER'S

I was bored too and said yes. We had to walk a city block to reach Rolando's cell, on the far side of the courthouse. When we got there, and saw him leaning on the bars, he seemed glad, too glad, to see us. "Oh," he said, "you guys, you guys were great!"

Though the cell had the same type of light as before, it now had lost its holy character, and now it seemed like the light I might turn on at work. Though the Nehru jacket still seemed weird.

Scott smiled at him. "They wake you up at three o'clock today?"

"Yeah," Rolando said.

Three in the *morning*? I stared. "You mean each day they wake him up—"

"Yeah," said Scott. "They have to wake him up at three to get him ready."

Why? Just a prison rule.

"He eats breakfast then too," said Scott. He turned to Rolando. "But you keep a roll with you, don't you?"

"Yeah," said Rolando.

"He puts it under his shirt."

"Yeah."

So he can eat a little throughout the day. No wonder he had seemed a little shaky. Maybe, who knows, Calvin had slept in later.

Now we started talking food. "After this," Rolando said, "I want to go out and celebrate! We'll go to dinner!"

It was creepy to think that in a few minutes a beeper could go off, and after seven years, bing, he's out of here forever. Or . . .

I didn't want to talk like this.

"We'll celebrate!" Then he dropped his voice as if a guard would overhear. I felt bad to hear him talk like this, but how could I stop him?

"What, uh, are these restaurants like?"

"Oh, I like—," Scott said, and then he named a place I hate. I was amazed how natural Scott could be with him. And so I decided to lighten up. Come on, talk to the poor guy, huh?

"The greatest restaurant in the city is Charlie Trotter's," Scott said. "That's a four star."

Rolando was nodding, so now I jumped in.

"Yeah," I said, "and if you're really special, they let you eat in the kitchen!"

Rolando was nodding, very serious, as if this were a class.

"Yeah," said Scott, "but for that they charge four hundred dollars a person."

Rolando seemed confused, happy, all at once.

"Yeah," I said, "and there's a big scandal. The city inspector from Sanitation, he won't let them eat in the kitchen. Says it's not sanitary!"

Rolando was laughing. With us.

"Yeah, it was a big incident," Scott said.

So now I was into it. Why be a prude. Suppose the worst did happen. So? He'd forget this part. The fiancée, she'd marry someone else. He already knew: "Your life isn't promised to you." It's what a black child was once quoted as saying to a writer, and it stuck with me be-cause . . . when I was young, I thought my life *was* promised to me.

Actually, if you're in prison, your life is, in a way, promised to you. Later, Scott would tell me a story how he did win an acquittal once for a young kid. And a week or so later, on the street, the kid was killed.

"Just in the past few months," Scott said, "the cops have shot, killed, maybe about ten kids." So in that way you could be better off in prison, though you're really better off if you have a table at Charlie Trotter's.

27. SCOTT'S BEEPER GOES OFF

I got into trouble after we said good-bye to Rolando and I stepped back into court. Though I'd been told how to come through this door, I now did it "the wrong way."

"Go through the JURY BOX!" a guard snapped. Damn! I'd forgotten that if I walked outside the jury box, a prisoner could grab, choke me.

Want to be a hostage?

"Gotta remember," said Scott.

Out in court it was dark, but the fiancée, I saw her. But there were two other shadows, and they were . . .

Lieutenant B.

Detective M.

But why? They were "done" yesterday. And later I would wonder, "Had they been sitting here all day?" How weird.

Both had their heads down. Lieutenant B. looked as if he was praying the rosary. I should have sneaked up and said, "Go away will you? He isn't dead yet."

But for the first time I wondered if they felt sorry for Rolando. But why spend the whole day here? As a taxpayer, I'm curious.

At this point, I still thought Rolando would be acquitted. A half hour went by. Then Scott and I began walking toward the south end of the building, and when we'd gone a distance—

Scott's beeper went off. . . . *Ah, he ran to the phone!* He called . . . and put down the phone, and walked back with an odd look:

"The jury has a question."

Uh-oh. Also I was pissed. What, they think this is a game? In law school, I hated kids with "questions."

"What do you think the question is?" I said. Scott and I were walking fast.

"I don't know."

Yes, how would he know? Ah, I'd been predicting to myself that by now they'd let Rolando go. We took the elevator, got off at six, and when we half jogged into court, already ahead of us and waiting, was Ms. M. And Mr. S. was there. And they had a look, as if:

There's a crisis in our family.

What is it?

Ms. M. looked grave and gave Scott a note, which had the question, in writing. Only when I saw the note, there were two questions, one handwritten in a big sprawling style and the other that was small and neat. The big sprawling question was:

"CAN WE CONVICT HIM OF ONE CRIME BUT NOT THE OTHER?"

Then the little question, in neat writing:

"If he has a juvenile record, may we see it?"

But I reacted to the big fat question. OH . . . SHIT! I knew it was bad luck to talk about Charlie Trotter's. Ah. And I turned and paced. Damn it. That question meant the jury would convict Rolando not of murder but of armed robbery. "Can we convict him of one crime, etc." Nice question!

"Well," said Ms. M., "the answer's obvious."

Yes it's "obvious" . . . but what was it? I didn't know criminal law. When Scott put down the note, I took it and my mouth fell open in that stupid way that all my friends point out to me, and I read over and over that other, second question. How had I missed this?

"Scott, look at this."

He came over.

"See?" I held up the note. "Two people wrote on this! Look at the difference in the writing!"

He stared.

"See," I went on. "See this first question, 'Can we convict . . . ?' how it's in a big fat stupid handwriting? Obviously this person is not the foreman. Too dumb . . . and that's the *bad* question for us. But now look at the other, smaller, neat. It's more intelligent. The person who wrote *this* . . . this is the foreman, don't you see?"

Yes, I had figured it out! Except . . . so what? The smaller, neat question was pretty stupid too.

Now the Judge came out. We walked up like children.

"Okay," said Judge K. "How do we answer it?"

I looked around. No one spoke. But already Judge K. was writing out his note.

Which had his answer.

Which was:

"YOU HAVE ALL THE INSTRUCTIONS YOU NEED. CONTINUE YOUR DELIBERATIONS."

See, it was obvious. It turns out, this is what we've been telling juries ever since the trial of Socrates.

But still . . . I looked around at Scott, Ms. M. . . . *Weren't we going to answer them?*

Okay, I guess not.

Sad, to turn and see the girl, the "fiancée," sitting as if no one told her. Did she know? That stupid juror and his "CAN WE . . . ?" Ah! I felt so bad for her. After all this waiting. And what to say to Scott? He seemed, though, to take it okay. But just in case, to cheer him, I said, "It's better if he's convicted of just one crime and not two, isn't it?"

He said nothing.

Yeah, it was shitty.

In fact, I was mad! "Who," I said to Scott, "who on that jury . . . who turned on us?" And in my mind, I was already dragging jurors out of their little box, and one by one, in Judge K.'s office, I was pointing and saying, Okay, who is it? Is it you? Are you the fink? I wondered if even Mr. A., the rocker, with his long hair, could have turned. Because now it was clear, I didn't know any of them, did I?

And yet I still thought, Well, they could acquit.

Maybe a mistrial. So, did the jury have a "question"?

I was glad we hadn't answered it.

28. WE'VE LOST!

In elections long after people of normal intelligence say, "We've lost," I go into a rage, and say, "NO! I can see exactly how we can still win."

So at this point I was thinking, The jury can still acquit. Even when I know I'm breathing fairy dust, I'll go on hoping for a while. But then at two A.M., tonight, there'll come a voice from hell:

YOU LOST!!

That's what I was doing as I took a seat in court. Might as well stay. That's what Scott was doing. By now, Judge K. had moved on to another trial.

So I could watch. Sit. With Rolando's mom. With Detective M. With . . . well, the fiancée. And as a lawyer, I could now do what lawyers have done for centuries:

Sit and heeny-hawk at a trial I have no business watching.

But was this a trial? I didn't see a jury. But I'd noticed that down here P.D.s would often try a case without a jury, and they had a way of putting this: "Yeah, I benched the thing." It meant the P.D. had a murder too nasty for normal people.

"I benched the thing." How I'd love to say that once.

Anyway, the prisoner, he was a Latino, and he'd done something that was . . . as Judge K. said, "not nice."

What? We're not children, tell us.

A cop was testifying as to how he got the Latino man's statement, and how he was part of a "bottle-gang hangout."

"Now," said Scott, "there's a word for you . . . 'bottle-gang hangout.' "

Though I smiled, I'd have liked to say, "Scott, right now how can you be so calm!!" It seems the issue was: Since the "bottle-ganger" only spoke Spanish, how well did the cop understand? Though a quarter of Chicago is Spanish speaking, the Chicago police have no official Spanish interpreters. "It's outrageous," said Scott. So each time a Latino who speaks only Spanish confesses, there is a fact question as to whether even one of the Latino cops understood him. With this cop, the P.D. was now asking if he spoke Spanish in the *house:*

P.D.: Do you have children?

Cop: Yes. Daughter.

P.D.: Does *she* speak Spanish?

Cop: No.

I said, to Scott, in admiration, "That's a good question!"

P.D.: But you speak it at home?

Cop: Sometimes.

And so on.

The more I saw of the guy with no English, the more I wondered, Does he even speak Spanish? He had a look so Indian.

Did he speak at all? He had a look so angelic, or from another world.

Now there was a break, and the P.D. just stopped. As if by a pre-arranged signal, she and the Judge and the State's Attorney went to the back. A deputy took the Latino, or Indian, away.

I went up, and on the defense counsel's table were big color photos. Glancing, Scott pointed to one: "This is where he grew up. Gorgeous, isn't it?"

Gorgeous?

A photo of a man, walking in a forest that was . . . Paradise. It was green. Maybe too green even for the Spanish poets.

And there was a path that went by a river, and the river was so blue! It's like Paradise, I kept thinking.

So how could a man who was in Paradise end up here, in this case, for doing something . . . well, "not nice"? It made me think of what someone says of Nature. . . .

It's Saint Paul, I think. How Nature itself is groaning, the Green of this "Paradise" is groaning, how the Spirit in Everything is groaning, and calling out, to be redeemed! I shivered. I wanted to think about something else.

"Where is everyone now?"

"They're back in chambers," Scott said. "And the P.D., she's doing what a P.D. does."

"What?"

"You go back there and try to find out if the judge is going to kill your client. Now, if he seems to say, 'Look, if I find him guilty, I'm not going to kill him,' then . . . you may want to waive the jury."

"I see."

I didn't. I was still staring at the man, in paradise, walking down a dusty road. But Scott said we could go back into the Judge's chambers and listen. I was amazed that we could just walk in. I couldn't imagine walking into the office of a U.S. District Court judge, and saying, "Hi, Your Honor, I just thought I'd come back here in your chambers, don't mind me, you go on." My God, I'd be shot. But I followed Scott in.

No one even noticed. I saw the P.D. from court. She was with a State's Attorney.

The P.D. was a white middle-aged woman, and she was a true P.D., in that she was wearing a Navaho blanket. Yet she looked like what Scott said she was: i.e., the daughter of two Protestant missionaries. She was from a small town in I———. How had she ended up doing this grisly work?

She and the State's Attorney seemed to get along, and they both talked very fast, and I caught snatches like:

"First, this defendant . . . first he slugged her."

"That was the foreplay," said the other.

"That was the foreplay!"

"Then he dragged her around the room, and now we get to the sex part—"

"Which wasn't easy," the other broke in. "Because they kept knocking over the glue bottles. . . ."

"But anyway then we get to the cutting . . . !"

And when we got to the cutting, I had to leave, for air. Both of the lawyers, by the way, were women.

But I stopped . . . no, I was curious. They were discussing the victim's age. A prostitute, she had been raped, and then murdered, then mutilated . . . how old was she?

"Well," said one of the women lawyers, "we know this, Judge . . . she isn't getting any *older!*" Both the women began to laugh.

Then it occurred to me, surgeons must talk this way.

Maybe not.

Up in the Loop, in federal court, or in my world, no lawyer would talk this way, even in a tort case. But federal or "my" court is a court of President Clinton, of Washington, D.C., of lawyers who read *The New York Times.* No one up there would say, "She's not getting any older!"

Yet while I may look down on Twenty-sixth and Cal, I learned, to my shock, that a few lawyers would say state court is more "civilized." Or they prefer it. Federal court? It's . . . well, fascist. But aside from the cold, black and white, Duchess of Malfi look of the court. To a defense lawyer like Scott, a federal court means:

No bail. No bond. Can't get the client out.

I used to think if you couldn't get bail, it must be very serious, and once upon a time in this country it was true. Only now, at least in federal, some lawyers say that virtually everything is no-bail, or no-bond. "In federal," Scott would say to me later, "if I can get bail in one case out of twenty, I'm doing great."

"And," I said, "why's it better to get bail?" (Other than being out.)

"All the studies show," he said, "if you're out on bail, your chances of winning go up."

I hate, hate to admit that a state court can do anything better. "So you think a state court is better?" I said.

"Sure. In state, your bond could be fifty to two hundred thousand dollars. . . . It depends, in a drug case, is it a kilo or how much?"

He paused. "You know how it works? You put up ten percent in cash."

"Yes." (I didn't know.)

But then it hit me: "You mean, kids are in jail down here because no one can post ten percent of a bond . . . like maybe a few thousand bucks?"

"Sure. Plenty of 'em."

Well, that's barbaric. But now I was rattled because I hate the states, and love the feds. Is it possible things are so bad in our country that . . . Cook County could seem good? I think of Washington, D.C., as civilization. But down there who now makes the law? The South. The West. That's where people are now. Texas. The Rockies. That's why in federal court now there isn't any bail.

Yes, maybe I'm wrong to look down on Twenty-sixth and Cal. A little wrong. Maybe when the two lawyers laugh, I should think of it as the laugh of liberty. The laugh of freedom.

There's bail, isn't there? I mean, when the day ever comes that families in this country have the money to post the bonds.

29. THE JURY HAS A QUESTION

We left the women laughing, and went back into the court, and a quarter of an hour later Ms. M. came up: "The jury has a question."

"Again?" said Scott.

Uh-oh, I thought.

Ms. M. had it.

"What? What is it?"

It was a paper scrap, which she gave to Scott.

Uh-oh.

Scott read, then passed it to me. In a new hand, a message: "WHAT IF SIX SAY HE'S GUILTY AND SIX SAY HE'S NOT?"

Ms. M. smiled, shook her head. So did Mr. S. And Scott said, "I've never known a jury with so many questions."

Judge K. was on the bench now, and this time he did not call us. Already he was writing his answer:

"YOU HAVE ALL THE INSTRUCTIONS YOU NEED TO DECIDE. CONTINUE YOUR DELIBERATIONS."

What, we're the Oracle of Delphi? Why can't we just answer? Ah no, this is how it's done. Rolando was out. Why? It was his "right," to be "present." Someone had to drag him back. (Did the jury know that each time it had a stupid question, a guard hauled out the kid?) Now I looked at Scott, and he was beat. It was over, wasn't it? That's it. Six to six. It was going to be a mistrial. After all that work! But I think he was relieved. From the questions of the jury, I guess he was afraid they would come back with a "Guilty."

Still I hoped: In five minutes they'd be back. Not Guilty. Because a computer could, etc., etc.

Well, I'd said that.

"No," said Scott. In fact, the delay, at first, hadn't bothered him. "It's easy to find them Guilty. It's much harder to find 'em Not Guilty."

Anyway, it seemed like it was over. Why didn't Judge K. let us go home and eat! In the car, I'd tell Scott, "You were great. The closing," etc. What's more, unlike Ms. M. and Mr. S., he only gave one. But I was too tired to talk now. Damn jury. I still had the idea that if the jury could have just watched this show, our side would have won. In that sense TV was good for us. But probably TV was bad for us: Thanks to TV, their brains'd gone to rot.

Ah, I was pissed. Then I turned over the piece of paper with the last message. I read it twice. "Look," I said to Scott. I handed him the slip. "They didn't say it *was* six to six. They said, What *if* it's six to six?"

But Scott waved this off. No, by now, he wanted a mistrial. He was right. We couldn't risk it. Let's say that it *was* six to six: How likely were "our" six to cave? I got a mental cramp thinking about the six to six: what was the fault line of the split?

Sex?

Jury was now six men, six women. We must have the women. Now in a calmer moment I would scoff. A friend who does polling tells me, "The gender gap? Isn't any. Women in the country are going the same way as the men. It's just, they're doing it more cautiously."

Not the ones who read *Ms.* But the others.

Yes, if it's the women, they'll definitely cave. Like in Germany, in 1933, when they elected Hitler. "Bob loves Hitler, and I just want some peace in the house, etc." But I thought of another way the jury might have split.

Education?

The high school v. the college grads. To my shame, I, a snob, thought the college grads must be with us. A computer, etc. And why else had Ms. M. struck the CEO from the burbs? So if we had the smarter ones . . . I wanted to tell Scott, "Wait, we're going to win."

Now when I look back, the jury was split six to six, the way the country was later, over Bush v. Gore. Maybe that was the split. In a certain way, that split had something to do with education. The day before the vote, I saw a poll, in *The New York Times* that showed where Bush and Gore had their support. Among the poor, high school grads, Gore was in the lead. (But they don't vote.) More important, Gore held his own with college grads and postgrads. So where in here did Bush do well?

White males with . . . "some college." Like the guys we'd sent to Vietnam. That's where Bush blew Gore away. As my friend Bill in construction said when we talked about this poll, "The very guys who are being fucked the most by the Bush crowd. That's what's so pathetic."

What's pathetic is that when Clinton came in, his big idea was: Send more guys to college. Why, so they'd come out more pissed than ever? With "some" college. Many are making less. Luckily, the wives work.

Great, then they really vote for Bush! Probably on this jury, fuming, they're voting to get Rolando.

No, what's pathetic . . . and, Bill, you're the one who told me . . . is how these types of guys in the 1960s would get "fucked around" by us. By us, who went to the real college. It's a point I came upon, yes, if I can say it, in Montesquieu. About being "above the law." No republic, he said, can last for long if any group's above the law. Wasn't that true for me, my friends? The reality was, we wouldn't be drafted. So we began by knowing we were "above the law." Or at least the draft law, which is the only law that mattered.

Yet I went on reading, eating cookies, and thinking Equality Was All the Rage. Oh, well, as friends say, I may overestimate how important "class" is. With this jury, I suppose, it all comes down to race.

Attitude to race?

If Rolando were black, he'd have been dead from the start. If white, he wouldn't be here. So maybe the split is that, color-wise, he's in the middle.

That's what's so maddening. It could really go either way. Possibly, the blacks on the jury are for Rolando. But it's also possible the blacks on the jury are against him too.

Maybe both races. A friend who's Latino, a business type, once said to me that both blacks and whites distrust Latinos.

"Why?" I said.

He smiled. Superior.

"Because we can have sex with anyone."

Anyway it was depressing. Right now the one hope was a mistrial.

30. THE JURY HAS ANOTHER QUESTION

It was now long after six P.M. when Scott came over to say, "The jury has a question." Ms. M., Mr. S. came over too.

"Now what?" someone said.

What is it with them?

Out stumbled Rolando. I was scared for him now, and like Scott, I wanted a hung jury now. Yet I admit one keeps hoping. Maybe we can still win it.

Judge K. climbed up, but instead of reading a question, he spoke directly: "They've asked if they can see a transcript of Calvin ————'s testimony."

"No!" said Scott. It was the first time I'd seen him annoyed. This surprised me because . . . why shouldn't the jury see it? But after Scott, came Ms. M.:

"No."

Then Mr. S.: "No." From the Gangbangers Lounge, it seemed, one could hear the voices rising, No. *No!* It was like a chorus, which was coming now from every lawyer, the living and the dead, from the

S.A.s and the P.D.s, and this chorus seemed to grow. No! No! *No reading in the court!* Want to "read"? Go to a law library! And Scott and Ms. M. and Mr. S. were so vehement, I thought the Judge would be the worst, and say something like:

"MEMBERS OF THE JURY! BY GOD YOU SHALL NOT READ! THIS IS A COURT OF LAW! NO READING IN THE COURT!"

But no, he was mild. "You know," he said, "the appellate courts up there, lately, they are getting pretty touchy about our not letting them read transcripts. If this jury wants a transcript, I think . . . we have to let them have it."

Voices rose. "No!"

"Judge . . . !"

But Judge K. said, "I think we have to." But now we had a problem. Had anyone typed up Calvin's testimony? No. And the court reporter who had taken it yesterday wasn't here today. She had taken the day off!

Nice woman. She had amazed me because she used lots of four-letter words, such as: "What a fucking mess this is. . . ." In fact her language was so foul, I thought at first she was a state's attorney.

But no, just a court reporter. Her successor, today, now piped up: "Judge, she told me last night, 'This trial, it's a mistrial, it won't be going—' " (Or words to that effect). Judge K. said, "Well, call her, get her right in." A deputy, nervous, phoned. "Judge, there's no answer!"

"We have any other number?"

"Judge . . ."

Uh-oh. He was going to blow up. No . . . he was going to send me! For a moment, that's what I thought. Send me in a squad car. "Find her!"

I pretended I had to go out for a moment, like to smoke a cigarette, which I'd never done.

•　　•　　•

I waited a minute, then came back. The Judge had made some decision, I could tell. What? Scott came over: "He's going to lock up the jury."

What? With Rolando?

No. Keep them overnight. Somewhere around here. Though every place around, it reminds you of the Bates Motel.

Scott shook his head. "In all my years as a P.D., I've *never* seen a judge 'lock up' a jury."

"Where are they going to stay?" I asked. But no one ever answered this.

Ms. M. was trying not to laugh. "Wait . . . wait till these jurors, wait till they find out they're going to be locked up."

"Yeah," said Mr. S., "are they going to be surprised."

Oh, did they want to see a transcript? Oh yes, they wanted to "read"? By God, they'll do it in the Bates Motel! The Judge told the deputy to keep trying the court reporter. "Get her in here tomorrow."

I was worried that once the twelve of them found they'd be held over, with no toothpaste, soap, and what cops'd let you take when they arrest you at home, then the jury would meet, on the spot, and say, "Wait! We find him guilty!" I doubted our six (all of them women?) would care enough about Rolando to stay here overnight. "I'm worried," I said to Scott.

"About?"

"They'll come out, right now, and say he's guilty."

But Judge K. went on writing out his order. They'd get their meals. No liquor, no drinking. They couldn't discuss the case, except in session. It was all right in the order.

Wait till they see that, I thought. I still bet we see a note. . . . "Wait, we find him guilty."

A few minutes went by. The jury sent out a note.

"Aha," I said to Scott.

Judge K. called us up. This time, without Rolando. "The jury," he said, "has a . . . question." I gulped.

No . . .

"They want to know," he said, "can I change my order, about not having any liquor?"

The judge paused. I assumed he'd say no. Or something like:

"YOU HAVE ALL THE LIQUEFACTIONS YOU NEED. CONTINUE YOUR BIBULATIONS."

But he hesitated. Come on, I thought, let them have a drink. Or two. I even tried to beam the idea of two up to him. Though later, I'd wonder if letting them drink was wise. Right now, it was our goal to get a mistrial. Letting them have a drink or two . . . it could lead to a verdict. There is a famous *pensée* by Pascal: "Too little wine, Man cannot find truth. Too much wine: same result." So two drinks were a risk. We didn't want them thinking late at night they'd hit the truth. Whether my beaming made any difference, the Judge now said, "I'll amend my order . . ."—he was writing as he spoke—". . . and let each juror have two drinks. But only two."

31. ABOVE THE LAW

So we left.

Perhaps we could not save Rolando. But we did lock up the jury! What a day. When we got on the elevator, we found a judge, a woman, African American. "Hi, Scott!" she said. "You on trial here?"

"Yeah, before Judge K."

"Oh?" she said. "Is it over yet?" (It was a joke that Judge K. went very fast.)

"It took three days."

She was shocked. "Three days? Before Judge K.?"

"Yes." And we all laughed. I don't know why I did.

Then out in the parking lot, we passed Mr. A.'s car. The rocker. Scott had seen him pull in that morning. It was sad to see that car, all alone. But it was fun, to think, "Hey, we locked him up!" It was fun to think that now as a lawyer I could go anywhere tonight. I could go to Reza's. Eat shish kebab. But Mr. A., the jury? No, and it gave me a little thrill to think: Suddenly, to be down here, with no toothpaste. For a single night . . . to foreswear the world!

Scott gave me a lift. Rush hour was long over. "Remember," he said, "when they asked Rolando, 'Oh, weren't you standing there at rush hour?' "

"I . . . sort of remember," I said.

"I bet Rolando doesn't even know what a 'rush hour' is."

We were stuck now, not moving.

"That's what gets me," I said. "Ah! He's back there . . . he's innocent! You know? It's the last thing I expected. . . ."

It wasn't, by the way.

" . . . the last thing, you know, that I'd come down here, and . . . you know, he's *innocent!*"

Scott paused in a funny way before answering. Then he said, "You know . . . I no longer find that an interesting question."

"What?" I said. "You don't find it interesting if he's innocent?"

He didn't answer directly. "I'll tell you what interests me. . . . 'What is it that can be *proved?*' "

Well, that's because he's a lawyer, and so am I, but I'm a second chair, so I didn't have to worry about "what can be proved." And as a civil lawyer, I'm more interested in "what can be settled." But what Scott said was remote to me for a bigger reason: that in this case, we shouldn't apply any "law" at all.

No, that's not right: in a way, I'm obsessed with applying the law. It's why I love to hide in a library. Soon I'd find the law I wanted to apply . . . which, as I've said too much, is the Convention on the

Child. Yes, it only urges, does not require, that we try Rolando as a minor. "If only it did 'require,' " a human rights lawyer once said to me. But this loophole is for countries too poor to have a juvenile court. But why rant like an idiot? My harping on international law . . . people start to think you're weird.

32. WHEN I BECAME "ADULT"

Of course we do have an unofficial "Convention on the Child," at least for some of our kids. It can even last to their midtwenties, I know that in my own life, one was in effect for me.

In terms of the draft, etc. But in other ways. During Scott's closing I had wondered, Could I ever have been in the "wrong place"? I'd have gotten lost along the way.

But I was also an adult early on, in ways kids aren't today. Just by virtue of being a Baby Boomer, people paid you a strange kind of attention.

Most of all I felt adult whenever I had a sense, in the 1960s, that as a kid, I was part of History. There are two, maybe three times I felt this in an eerie way:

Summer 1966

On a date, after a race riot. National Guard in jeeps. Shining spotlights on you and your date, under the elm of the front lawn. Or they said this happened to some kids. I was on the porch, and for the first time, trying to kiss a girl.

Do you think, she said, they're out there, driving around?

I was nervous. It was dark.

The adult thing to do was to kiss her and be shot.

June 1968

My wisdom teeth were being taken out, in a hospital. Later, under anesthesia I slammed into a wall. Concussion. When I came to . . . they said Robert Kennedy had been shot. Dead? No one knew. For at that moment, the hospital staff turned off the TV, no more news. It seemed 1968, as a year in history, was too upsetting to the patients.

I was furious. Got to a phone. Began calling my friends. Is Kennedy *dead?*

They'd cut off TV. I was there in my nightgown. I'd never felt so adult.

1967–71

College. Often we were treated as children. But in a strange way, the adults or the ones who read *The New York Times* seemed to look up to us.

Stop racism. Stop the bombing. Stop the war.

It was up to us.

Yet at other times, you might feel empty, since you had no role in this war at all. Our dads had all been to war. Why not us?

One night, at the school paper, we had a big meeting on an editorial. Would we, or would we not, support the Viet Cong, the NLF? The meeting went on, and on. I should have brought a toothbrush.

The whole night felt adult. Like a real council of war. Hour after hour I sat cross-legged on the floor. I was one of the minority arguing, "We can't support the Viet Cong." While I hated the war, how could we, out of the draft, vote in favor of . . .

Helping the guys shoot the kids we went to high school with!

It's funny, I don't blame the kids who voted for the Viet Cong.

It's . . . well, at that age, how I too wanted to be part of Something Bigger.

Finally, I think of a time when in college, a group of us were hauled in to howl at some famous alumni: a senator, a banker, a famous widow, maybe six in all. We were going to tell them about "The Mood on Campus." By luck I was the last to speak. So I went on a long, emotional jag about: Stop the War. Stop. Stop it now. At the very end, Give Me Liberty . . . or, I'd be upset.

When I sat down, I knew I'd shocked them. The alums said nothing. Or there was a long silence. Then one of the widows smiled in a bright way:

"Well! And how old are you boys?"

Now, why did she have to say that? It was a bitter thing to think that at this moment in my childhood, I was already twenty-two.

33. BIG DAY

At three A.M. while I slept the next day, a guard woke Rolando to dress, sneak a roll—then sit, for hours, in a tunnel to the court. Wait until he's counted, and collected, by the next guard. This can take as long as a flight to L.A. When I woke at seven A.M. I felt tired too. I put on Bach and then it hit me: I had no place to go today. I could not take a cab to Twenty-sixth and Cal. It was silly, as I was only second chair, to go down just to "wait." Yesterday it was all right. But now after my complaining I'd blush to go back. "Here I am to wait!" So I picked out my usual pinstripe suit for this day of the week. But I thought: Ah, Twenty-sixth and Cal, if only I could go back in disguise. Like Sir Richard Burton, in his travel narrative: in a sash, a white robe. How he slips into the Holy City. Perhaps I could do the same. But with all my downtown suits I'd be pointed out and shunned, as a "litigator," from the Loop, where no one ever tries a case (at least in federal, civil, etc.) That's what this navy blue suit of mine seemed to say. So I'd just dress as a P.D. Hop in a cab: just blow off the day. Waiting for Rolando's verdict. No one would even know me, and as Burton writes somewhere, for a whole day I'd be "truly orientally *lost.*" Oh, and bring a toothbrush, in case I'm locked up.

And a bit of baksheesh, for the Gangbangers Lounge.

Come on. This is serious. What about Rolando's verdict? Well, it's only eight o'clock. Jury won't come back at eight.

Anyway, I have to go to work. My real job.

Soon up on the El, I was staring meekly at *The Times,* and back in the real world. And I was amazed how, when this was the Big Day, etc., I was soon on the phone, sending letters—

I wasn't thinking of the jury.

I wasn't looking at my watch.

I wasn't thinking, "What if he's guilty. . . ."

But I left a message in Scott's voice mail, and he phoned. "It doesn't make sense for me to—" I started saying.

"No, it doesn't."

I was sorry he said this, but it was true. "Will you call me when the jury . . . ? I'll just jump in a cab, and . . ."

I'd never make it. Why pretend?

By the way, Scott was still saying, "There isn't going to be a verdict." Still, he must have hoped!

Or maybe I thought that, and read it in his tone of voice. I said, "I think there will be a verdict."

No reason. Just because Scott said the opposite. They teach you in law school, "If someone says one thing, you should say the opposite."

Anyway Scott said, "I don't know." Or, "I don't think so." Or, "I think it'll be a mistrial."

I asked if he would call back, just keep me up to date. And when we rang off, I went out to talk to D., my secretary, and tell her the Special Order of the Day, which was:

PUT SCOTT'S CALL THROUGH!

No matter what. Because he had a beeper but not a cell phone, and I couldn't call him back.

"Okay."

"No, not okay," I said. This was life or death. "Don't just put Scott into voice mail, okay? Please?"

"Okay!"

I have to say this because we have an office rule of never screening calls. No one ever says, "Who's calling?" And "I'll see if he's available." As if: I'm talking to Warren Christopher, and have no time for you. But if I am (because with no screening, a Warren Christopher can get right through to me), then for the caller there isn't any loss of face. "They don't know who I am." So for me to come out and say, "PUT SCOTT'S CALL THROUGH," was a big change. So I said again: "Okay?"

"Okay!"

All ships at sea. I'm serious.

Anyway, I went back to my "civil" cases, and they all seemed boring. Once over in federal court, a new judge who'd been a prosecutor said to us in chambers: "I don't know how you all do it, this 'civil' law. It's so boring!" He laughed at us.

I had to laugh too, because he was the judge.

I wish I'd said, "Your Honor, you know what's boring? It's to be a judge. Just sit up there, and never speak out, like we do. I don't know how all you judges do it!"

Years ago, an older lawyer told me, "The last thing I'd ever want to be is a judge." At the time I was shocked: Isn't that what we all want?

Now I know. "Judge." Awful thing, in a way.

In federal court, there's a judge I know of, and he was so bored that he began to write a screenplay. It was about a judge who is so bored during the criminal trials, etc., that he begins to plot the perfect crime. And then he decides to pull it off. Apparently, this screenplay was really good. But at the last step of approval at the studio, the people at the top decided to kill it. Why? No one told me.

Maybe in Hollywood they'd divided six to six.

I was trying to distract myself. It was ten A.M. No call from Scott. It was eleven A.M. and no call from Scott. I was amazed. I thought, after being locked up overnight, the jury would come right back and decide. Lunch, and no decision. I got a call from Scott: "Nothing. No decision."

Now he was sure there'd be a mistrial.

"Oh," I said, "I think there'll be a verdict." But now I thought, Scott is right.

Now it was about one o'clock.

Every time I was on the phone and saw a call coming in for me, I freaked out. But it wasn't Scott.

Now it was one thirty. Maybe I should just go down there.

No.

Now it was about two o'clock. What if he's guilty? I wonder what will happen to the fiancée.

Now it was about two thirty. Why did I think, purely on gut, there was going to be a verdict, one way or the other? Because, purely on gut, I bet on Clinton in '92. (No one else would, in May of that year.)

Now it was about three o'clock. While I'd kept my calls short, now I took a call and let it go much longer. We even started telling jokes. While I laughed, I saw the phone and how the message light was burning:

Red. I had a message.

Ah! How long had it been red? "I have to go," I said. But if it was Scott, I'd said to put him through, but I punched in my code, and the Dark Lady of the Sonnets said:

You

Have

. . . TWO . . .

Messages.

Ah! I hit the two (2) and zero (0) the first time, it was Scott! He was talking fast: "The jury, it's got a verdict! I can't wait! I'm going over!"

Which now meant, if I hit the star (★) and zero (0) this time, I'd get my second message: Scott, telling me the verdict.

So this would be: The Verdict. Funny, to see it burning red. And before I did the star (★) and zero (0), I now knew it would be Guilty. Guilty of one crime, but not the other: robbery, not murder. Because I knew with a new clarity: This is what they had been deadlocked over, as the first jury question said, "Can we convict him of one crime, and not two?"

Shit. Should I hit . . . ?

Don't. Just don't hit the star (★) and zero (0) . . . no, I *had* to hit it, I had to know, but SHIT, I was in a rage, when I hit the thing, and . . .

Not guilty. Well. There you go.

I felt . . . calm.

For a second. And then the word that boiled up was DAMN! I'd said, fifty times today, to put his call through! And now? I could have been there for the hugging, and the crying, and. . . . But no, couldn't I still get there, if I got in a cab? See Scott, and . . . No, I couldn't make it. Yes, I bet I could!

So out I went, screaming, till a cab stopped, and somehow by four o'clock I was running past the kids outside of court.

Oh, Twenty-sixth and Cal!

"NOT GUILTY!"

And I banged on the elevator, and now I was going up, and I wasn't mad at D. for putting Scott in voice mail, though I had said about fifty times. . . .

Ah, come on!

I kept hitting "6," for sixth floor, to make the thing go faster, and at last the door opened, and I ran . . . and ran . . . and burst into Judge K.'s court, and . . .

No one was there. No one. What?

No one in the back. No one.

Except two lawyer-looking types, who were speaking in a hush. I didn't know them. So I approached them.

"Do you know anything about Rolando ———?" I said his last name.

"Oh," said one of the young lawyer types. "You mean the 'Not Guilty'?"

"Yes, yes," I said. "The 'Not Guilty.' Do you know where he . . . where they are?"

The other young lawyer type said, "Why don't you go back in chambers. I think—everybody's gone. But I think the two State's Attorneys are back there."

Oh no.

Ms. M. Mr. S. What? Do I go back and high-five them?

Then I realized, the two young men were prosecutors because one of them said, "Yeah, that sure was a tough case."

Oh? I thought. Then why'd you prosecute?

I knew where they had gone. Charlie Trotter's, to celebrate. No, that was absurd. But some place not as pricey. I ran out to the pay phone and called Scott's office, to find out where they'd gone.

Rob, his partner, answered: "Why don't you go back to the jury room? That's probably where they are."

Huh. Didn't think of that.

But when I ran back, it was empty. Then I saw a guard: "Yeah, they're gone."

"Everyone?"

"You might catch 'em on the way out."

Yes, I ran downstairs, and my God, I saw a juror! It was the little man in the windbreaker: the administrative "judge." I caught up with him, and got in front of him, and smiled, and said, "Well . . . ! ! !"

He pushed around me, and I realized he was irked, and I knew he'd been voting Guilty. (But how did I know?)

"I wish," he said, "I sure wish they had told us they were going to keep us here last night!" And he was mad.

Then I saw another juror, the woman who had called the cops on her husband. (So she said, on voir dire.) And she was frowning, and pushing through. A voice inside me said, Better keep away.

Any others? No.

But the way the first two jurors scowled, the next might take a swing at me. Anyway, they were gone, and it was barely after four o'clock. And now I knew, this trip was just a waste.

And so I turned, and . . . there was a cop, standing in front of me. Blocking my way. And when I looked up at his face . . .

It was a she.

A woman cop. And she was gorgeous.

In her twenties. Long red hair. Like in a 1940s movie way, like Maureen O'Hara. She really looked good in blue.

And she stood right there, and was smiling, and she said, *"Well?"*

I just gaped at her. God, she was *gorgeous!*

"Well?" she said again. And her smile was even bigger now.

"WELL?" she said. " 'Not Guilty'! Huh?" And now she began to laugh. How did she know—?

"Don't you remember me? I was one of the deputies," she said.

Yes, I remember. I think. . . . Or hadn't I noticed her? " 'Not Guilty'!"
She laughed again. "Do you know how rare that is around here?"

"It is?" I said.

"Oh, that's something you don't see anymore!"

"No?" Of course, when had she seen it? She seemed about
twenty-two. (She was GORGEOUS! How had I not noticed her in
court?)

"Uh . . . say," I said, "do you know, like, where the . . . uh . . .
everyone went?"

"They went off to celebrate," she said.

"Oh." I had to shake off the idea of them entering Charlie
Trotter's. For an insane second, I was even a bit jealous of Rolando!
How he was twenty-two, and . . . oh, to be . . .

Never mind.

Anyway, he was gone. No one knew where. So for the first time
this week, I was down here all alone. And now the problem was: How
do I get back? Scott was not here with his car. I had no ride. No way
to get a ride. The 1940s movie star had wandered off. So I went up to
another deputy:

"Any way I can get a cab?"

He laughed. He told me that the nearest El was six blocks to the
north. "It's a *long* walk," he said.

When I'd heard Rolando was acquitted, in my joy my first
thought was how Scott had called this court "the Bastion of Democracy." He meant that down here, unlike in federal, the lawyers didn't
fuss, they "just did it." And unlike in federal, you could get a "Not
Guilty." But Twenty-sixth and Cal is a "bastion" in another way. It's
unapproachable. Dangerous.

In other words, no cabs.

And so I decided, "Okay, I'll walk it." And outside the "Bastion of
Democracy," I passed blocks of beat-up homes where people live in
basements. Is this what Rolando saw when he walked out the door? I

walked for twenty minutes. I walked past blocks of cars parked since 1959. So cold that when I passed a lighted bar, the third one or the fourth, I stopped in to get warm. The air in it made me sick. So I walked on, twenty minutes to the El stop. Another twenty for a train. As I waited in the cold, I wondered how Rolando saw it.

Freedom!

Yeah. He'd go up to North and Damen. Where the runaways like to go. So many pictures of the "Missing Children" in the juice bars. Somehow, the kids seem like a rock band, touring.

Freedom.

So for Rolando, too, now. Tonight, maybe he'll even go to Ear Wax, to check out the new CDs. It's amazing how even now in America you can still start over at twenty-two.

And this kid, he'll have a job, probably in a week. Maybe in a year or so, he'll even start doing "some college."

Chilling thought: He'll be for Bush.

At last I got back, and as soon as I sat down, Scott was on the phone. (Now they put him through!) I could hear kids laughing and shouting.

"Where are you?" I said.

Over the noise he tried to talk. "I'm . . . at a day care center!" Right after the verdict, he had to run, pick up his daughter. He just drove off.

I . . . I began to laugh. Charlie Trotter's, huh? This was like . . . winning the last game in the World Series, then rushing out to get to the Laundromat before it closed. "Yeah," said Scott, "I didn't even see the jury."

"I did," I said. "Or I saw two of 'em." Which was enough. "Tell me," I said, "when you got over, what was happening?"

"When I got over," said Scott, "Rolando was going nuts! A guard had come by and told him, 'It's Not Guilty.' So I said, 'Wait, sometimes those things are wrong. Don't get so excited!'"

But it was far from wrong, and I laughed. It all had come out fine.

And it was connected to the fact Scott could now be helping out at day care. The self-possession of a lawyer to do this, when I'd be too self-intoxicated to move. . . . Scott, how could you be so calm?

Because the lawyer is on trial. That's, in part, who they vote to acquit.

34. A JUROR SPEAKS

After dithering—for about two years—I phoned up a juror to ask how they voted. I picked out a man I'll call Mr. Y., who had seemed to be the most "liberal."

"What?" he said. "That was a long time ago, wasn't it?" But we'd talk in a week, and I said something nice about him being a "liberal." A week later when I called, he said, "You thought I was a liberal?" He paused and said:

"You were lucky there were a lot of women." Uh-oh. "Why did you think I was a liberal? Oh I know. . . ." He figured that out.

"So," I said, "that's how it broke, the six to six? I thought maybe . . ." And then I told him how Ms. M. had struck the guy whose dad had the gas station because he might be Jewish. "Who," said Mr. Y., "made those decisions? I assumed the defense attorney made all those decisions."

I was surprised. "No, Ms. . . . both sides did." I then asked if maybe the split was based on education. "You know, college grads would say, 'Acquit,' and high school . . . they'd say—?"

"You mean intelligence?"

"Well," I said. "No. . . ."

But this nettled Mr. Y. "If you were intelligent, you knew he was guilty." Then a pause, "Of course if you were . . . very intelligent, you could see it in a broader perspective. So in something like this, intelligence . . ."

He paused. So I volunteered: "You mean, intelligence . . . it was like a wash."

"You might say."

But I still had not asked Mr. Y. how he had voted, and we were on the phone too. So that's another reason why both of us were circling, probing. "So," I said, "it was women. That was the breakdown."

He now backed off a little. "Women played a role." Then he added something: "They were mostly suburban."

I didn't remember that.

". . . And from the nicer suburbs. New ones. Affluent."

No! I thought of that woman from Lincoln Park. "You sure about the suburbs?"

"Yeah," Mr. Y. said. "I assumed from the nicer suburbs. They had to travel pretty far."

Well, if they're from Lincoln Park, they have to travel pretty far. How had I gotten Mr. Y. so wrong? And if I got this wrong, maybe I have everything about the case wrong. Anyway, I now asked about the principal: He, I knew, wanted to convict.

"Who?"

"The principal?" I said.

"The older gentleman?"

"Yes."

"He was against," Mr. Y. agreed.

"He seemed like a hard guy." I said this to provoke.

"He was a good guy."

Long pause.

"I suppose you realize now I was against you," said Mr. Y.

"I *do* realize that." I laughed. (I might as well laugh.)

"And you thought I was a liberal." He sort of laughed. Except I did think, in a way, even now, he was sort of a liberal. But in a very weird way.

So why was he—?

But let me ask him. "So why, why didn't you . . . I mean vote to acquit? Why?"

"Why?" he said. "I wasn't convinced. That's why I held out so long."

Oh God, I called exactly the wrong guy. I should have called one of the women. But I had thought they might freak out.

"And," Mr. Y. was going on, "your whole thing about coercion, it seemed so . . ."

"What?"

"It seemed so underhanded," he said.

UNDERHANDED? But I stayed calm. "What do you mean, 'underhanded'?"

"I even said that in the jury room. . . . I didn't mind letting him go. But not this way. It was underhanded."

I had to tell myself, Keep calm, keep your temper, anyway he was acquitted. So I tried to explain to Mr. Y., and I still liked him, that the defense of "compulsion" wasn't underhanded, it was . . . Well, if we couldn't raise it, then he'd never have gotten a second trial, and Rolando would still be in jail today. Did he know that? I blabbed on, and on.

Then I remembered: I'm supposed to ask questions. "So you didn't buy the coercion thing . . . ?"

"No."

"What about Calvin's testimony? You know, the older kid?"

"How could you believe it? He didn't have anything to lose."

"My God . . . ," I said, forgetting I was interviewing. "You thought Calvin didn't have anything to lose?"

"He was just helping a friend."

"A friend?" I said. "They were different ages, different race. . . ."

"They could have been friends," said Mr. Y.

"Could have been? You're going to convict on that?"

Ah, why was I arguing with this guy? Anyway I tried to explain the risk Calvin was running, how Scott had warned him, etc. I was so upset with him that now I regretted making the call. Bitter, I even said, "So, who was the champion against him?" That is, Rolando.

That is: Mr. Y., was it you?

"There wasn't any champion against him."

Yes, that was a stupid thing for me to say. And remember, this guy had voted to acquit. Okay, I was ashamed too. Besides, he had his reasons.

Yes, what were they? I was now depressed, but I asked him anyway.

"I could look at him!" Mr. Y. said. "I knew who he was."

"How'd you know who he was?" I said.

"I didn't think he was a jellyfish. He was in that Raiders uniform."

What? I paused. "What Raiders uniform?"

"They had a picture of him in the lineup. He was in a Raiders uniform."

He meant the gang colors. But where Rolando grew up, the White Sox were selling jackets, T-shirts, in the same gang colors. Ah, that pissed me off, not against Mr. Y., but against all the White Sox owners, Jerry Reinsdorf, etc., who went around marketing gang colors. Then the kids buy the gang colors.

And next? Some kid is serving forty years. But I was really mad, because I totally missed the photo when Ms. M. had handed it to the jury. So much for being a second chair.

But Mr. Y. had voted to acquit! So why? Why, if he thought Rolando—? But now, moving on, Mr. Y. was blasting every jury, or at least any that'd ever voted to acquit. "Certain people . . . ," like the women, he implied, "they're living in these 'cushy' places and watching TV. They don't see the nitty-gritty. . . ." He paused. "You know, a lot of people, they don't want to *deal with it*. . . ."

(Yeah? Maybe some thought, Rolando shouldn't have to either.)

"You know what got me?" said Mr. Y. "We weren't a jury of his peers. . . ."

(Huh?)

"People don't know what it's like to have your life threatened. . . . Our mind-set is: I have food, I have my 'cush' life. . . . Who am I to make someone so miserable?"

(Who? Exactly.)

By now this call was fatiguing both of us. But I couldn't end it, and it's odd how I knew, Mr. Y. can't end this either. By now I stopped pretending it was an interview. The two of us were just arguing.

"But," I said, "you *did* acquit. Why? That's what I want to know, why?"

Yes, why? Oh, various things. Various things. Factors. That weighed on him.

Me: Like the fact he was so young?

Mr. Y: (Pause) Yes. He was so young.

Of course that weighed against Rolando too, since Mr. Y., like every man, was once a little wild, though "not like that."

"Did the jury know," I asked, "that he had been in jail?"

"Yeah," he said, "we couldn't figure that out." The jury knew that Rolando had been in a kind of jail. (How? I was surprised that they knew.) "But," said Mr. Y., "it was like a juvenile prison, wasn't it?"

He sounded, for once, not sure. And now I knew I had him. "No," I said, slowly. "It was an *adult* prison."

He was silent. Ha. I'd rocked him, a bit. "It was an adult prison," I said again, and "maybe that's why he didn't look like such a, you know, jellyfish. . . ."

"I could see the way he looked right now," snapped Mr. Y.

"He'd been in prison for seven years!" I said.

"People don't change that much!" he said.

"Sure they do!"

And now, breathing hard, we stopped. And Mr. Y. told me what the jury'd done that night. At the break it was fifty-fifty, and the next morning, even before people met, it was somehow in favor of acquittal: nine to three. What happened? A dream? "Now they started dropping like flies," Mr. Y. said. "People wanted the easy way out."

But Scott and most others say that the easy way out is to convict. "It's much harder to acquit them."

"It was a taxing thing," said Mr. Y. "Nobody wanted to say, it's just a human thing." I didn't understand any of that, so I said, for the tenth or so time now, *"But why did you acquit?"*

Why?

"Wouldn't you," he said, "rather fault on the side of not keeping him there the rest of his life?"

I found out, by the way, that to some on the jury, the two blacks (the UIC kid and the teacher) seemed to "sit it out." This may be why the UIC kid had his head down. He felt, as I did, that the whole thing was ridiculous.

35. A FINAL MEAL

What happened to Rolando, etc.? A few days after the verdict, I happened to talk to Scott, and he cleared up one thing I'd been confused about. "Yeah," he said, "I talked to Rolando, you know . . . what it's been like. He said about the first meal . . . when he got out, he doesn't really remember much about it. But his *second* . . . they all went to a Burger King. 'And Scott,' he said, 'I ordered a hamburger. And oh . . . I tasted that, I ate it, I ate it slooooowwww, and oh, oh, did that ever taste good!' "

We were both silent a second.

So that was it. A Whopper.

"God help us," I said.

"Yeah," said Scott.

Burger King, of course. They took him as a child, didn't they?

Speaking of which: The night after Rolando was acquitted, he still was locked up. Yes, after the jury found him "Not Guilty," a deputy grabbed him and dragged him back to jail and shut him in his cell. *Yes, he went back to jail.* Because the jail needs an order to let him go, and besides, there's no procedure over there to handle an acquittal. In a way, though, *was* it so bad? It may have been stranger if Rolando had, that minute, just walked away. Suppose after seven years, a guard had said, at the instant of acquittal, "Go. Come on. Go. Out the door. *NOW!*"

Still, it was an outrage to send him back. But . . . while I don't believe that "prison," or "the state" can be a living-breathing thing, it's as if "prison," which had raised this boy and now had to let him go, needed one more night to hold him in its arms.

Anyway, Scott got him out.

That's right, baby. HE'S OUT OF THERE! (Did I say that yet?) The great thing about being a lawyer, I think, is that while it is much more than "just a job," there is a moment sometimes when it *is* just a job, as in: Damn it come on, let's just get this kid out!

I can see how you may want to do it as a matter-of-fact, offhand thing. The way Scott said at the end:

"That's why you go to law school."

I suppose. To do a trial like this: in our time, I'm sorry to say, that *is* why you go to law school. And I began to wonder after this case— How could I tell a young law student today to look away from this and be a civil lawyer like me?

Part Two

"That's Why You Go to Law School"

36. WHAT I TRIED AFTER ROLANDO

When we start to see children in dreams, it's supposed to mean, says a ghost in *Jane Eyre,* that we are deeply unhappy. If I did not see children in mine after this trial, it may just mean I was unhappy already. Oh, I knew I didn't belong at Twenty-sixth and Cal, but I did want to do a new kind of law. But what? Bring back unions? No hope of that. Congress would have to do it. What could I do? I was proud of what I did as a labor lawyer, but it has so little to do with one frightened kid being in a cell. Ah, damn it! It's frightening how short a time we have to live. No motions to extend my time!

I was not sure what I could do as a civil lawyer, but whatever it was I had to do it fast. For years I realized I had been slowing down. Doing the same civil suits, over and over.

Race.

Sex.

Age.

I can file them over and over, and without unions in place, none of them do anything to raise wages. Or slow down inequality. When I was in college, the income of families in the top 5 percent was eleven times that of families in the bottom fifth. Now? The ratio has shot almost to twenty. Soon it may be higher still. And as a labor lawyer, I know I'm helpless to do anything about it.

Anyway, I wanted to do something that wasn't "labor," like: well, public interest law, I guess. It's something that as a union lawyer I had often scoffed at. Big suits to change the world? Nobody did that anymore, did they? But after Rolando and all that, I began to realize, Yes, I too am scared. Middle aged, I didn't have much time left. So why not file a few big cases? Beat on my little drum. We all want to feel, Oh, for a moment, at least I lived!

It's strange, though, that just to "do good" can be a matter of luck. Fortuna. Chance. The other day a lawyer friend of mine who's tried but had no luck at this said, "So now I'm just doing commercial cases. I look around at other lawyers, and wonder, What am I adding to the mix?"

It's luck to add anything. In a way, this is enraging, because I'm not even trying to make money. Doing good should be the consolation prize, shouldn't it? I once read, long ago, in Aristotle, that the highest good is happiness. And for a lawyer, he says, your particular happiness is not to get a big salary, but to bring about justice. But alas, says Aristotle, it turns out justice or my particular happiness is not in my control. That's why he tells us: Be a philosopher, you're independent. If you want justice, you depend on a lot of other people, like Mr. Y., Judge K., even Ms. M. Even more disturbing, in my case, I depend on who's appointing judges. I have to depend on President Bush.

But I want to be happy! And I figured that maybe luck would be a lady if I didn't care about the money. But there is a little problem. While I'm out there "doing good" and not caring about money, how, as a lawyer, am I going to get paid?

I know that I *should* start with what the cases were, and why they would make a difference. Or I suppose I should take up the cat calls from the Right, such as: (1) "Oh, more judicial activism?"; (2) "That era is over"; (3) "You can't use the courts for social change," etc.

But while all that is very serious, it's pretty minor compared with: How am I going to get paid? I am in a small three-lawyer firm, which in Chicago is like a mom-and-pop grocery store. That is, we're not even big enough in this town to be a "small firm." *"Small"* is fifteen. Years ago, a young associate of ours left, and before closing the door, he turned and said, wistfully:

"You know, it's very romantic, I suppose, being in these small firms. But the problem is, you can never leave!"

And the other problem is, as lawyers in small firms, we have to keep thinking about money. Right after Rolando's case, two lawyers, who are my age, and romantics just as much as I (though they would deny this), took me out for dinner. And we began to talk, as small-firm lawyers do, about money, money, money.

Earl said, "Rule number one . . . no more contingency cases."

That's right, no more cases where we go years and years without a fee.

"That's right," said Tom.

"That's right," I said. No more. As Chief Joseph of the Nez Percé said, we will bring these cases no more forever. I nodded.

"YOU!" said Earl, looking at me.

"Me?"

"You!" He pointed at me. "What *you* need is an institutional client." He meant like a bank, a building, a union, a thing, which by the hour I could bill and bill.

"That's right," said Tom.

"I can't believe," said Earl, "you've gotten this far without one." Because clients who are *people*, it's hard to bill them by the hour. Clients who are people, human, they have ears and little noses. How can you bill them by the hour, when they just look up at you with their little eyes?

"You mean," said Tom, "you have no institutional clients? How do you do it?"

"I . . . I don't know," I said.

"Well," said Earl, "no more contingency cases . . . that's the rule."

And we all nodded. And yet within *five* minutes Earl and Tom began to talk about how they might bring a big contingency-type case, which involved suing on behalf of the Navaho. A case, as I could fathom it, that would take at least twenty years.

I cut in, "Stop! We're too *old* to talk like this!"

And only a few minutes ago, it had been Earl, scowling, who

pointed at me: "You!" Yeah, well I'm not sitting here talking about bringing suits for the Navaho! But Earl, Tom, oh, deep down, I know: *it's just that we want to live!*

How I'd love never to send another bill: even to a building! I thought this the other day when I had lunch with Y. He was saying, "You don't like being a lawyer do you?"

Uh-oh. What was coming?

"I do," he said. "I like everything! Except . . . *one* thing!"

"What's that?"

"Clients!"

Now I was shocked. "But that's the only part of law I like!"

"Well, I hate mine!"

"Why?" I was amazed.

He looked at me, as if: Come off it! Then he said, "Billing them! Getting them to pay!"

Then I knew what the problem was: Unlike me, he had corporate clients. But sometimes these "corporations" are just human beings in disguise: a CEO who can only take you out to Wendy's. I've done this once or twice. We pretend we're big lawyers, like Kirk-land and Ellis. They pretend they're real companies, like Royal Dutch Shell, who can pay us. Then, when this all turns out to be a lie, on both sides, each side begins screaming, "I hate you, I hate you!"

Anyway, if I want to do good in the world, how do I get the money? And after years of thought, I know of only two ways:

1. Become an academic.

I hear at the big schools, you can get a hundred thousand dollars! And for some, that's just what they bank. Teach a class or two a week. Then you have the rest of the week just to practice law! Do slip-and-fall cases, if that's what you want.

To a friend of mine, I like to moan: Ah, but nobody would hire me! Except a law school, in El Paso, to teach a clinic, in a gulch, for about thirty thousand dollars.

"Have you applied?"

"No."

"Come on! You have to take a concrete step!"

But I'm too old! And what, does he want to send me up to Nome, Alaska? Besides, I don't want to teach even in the lower forty-eight.

The few times, by accident, when I'm back in a law school, and walk down a hall, I get ill, just to see it, full of kids, who, to me, are carriers of a disease, by which I mean the *longing*, all that longing. It makes me panic: that I'll be infected, by the longing! I want out. I have to leave. And though I know that I'm too old now for that longing, and that old people aren't infected, I don't even want to see it on the faces of these kids. Go back to law school? I'd walk around and remember: When J. and I broke up, and when . . .

Wait, I'm getting this mixed up with college. Anyway, the point is, I'd prefer to be in the Loop and billing people than being around these kids.

Besides, there's a second way I might get money, to allow me to go off and do good.

2. Bring a big class action, settle, and take a percentage as my fee.

Spend a few years in a big class action, a real gusher. Like the tobacco case. Stock fraud. Then, if it's a big award, the idea is not to ask for "my hours" but take a percentage, like a third, of the money you have won for the class.

Now in the 1980s the Reagan judges at first tried to take away the honeypots, i.e., my right to have a third. If you won, you would only get your hours, at your hourly rate. But just as they retreated on sanctioning us under Rule 11, they retreated on this as well, and now I can get a third.

But how do I find a case like this?

"Read the *Wall Street Journal*," older lawyers used to say. But apart from the fact that the editorials make me sick, I don't read the paper till lunch, and by then the good cases are gone. But for years I'd tell an older lawyer friend that one day I'd find such a case, etc. He'd listen, then say:

"Stop talking fantasy!"

But if I really need to raise money, isn't there one, final, last resort for us public interest types?

37. ASK SOROS

I could ask Soros. Or Ford. I could get a grant. And, I should add, I already had a case that I could raise money for, and I had been work- ing on it even before Rolando's trial. A group of lawyers, including me, had wanted to sue makers of handguns, under a "common law" theory of public nuisance. And after the trial, I now did believe what the other lawyers were saying: that the manufacturers had created a culture of gun use among minors, under age eighteen, and that one kid had to arm himself against the next kid.

But did that constitute a public nuisance?

At the time I worked on it, no city, no one in fact, had ever brought such a case. And while there may never have been a case quite like this, we had never before had an industry arming children: (1) They overproduced; (2) put no check on retailers; (3) made for- tunes on "straw" purchases.

Now I admit, public nuisance has not been used in the past for guns in the hands of children. But in the past, the kids didn't have the guns. Rent the movie of *West Side Story:* the kids in those gangs are still using knives.

Nuisance in the time of Sir Edward Coke was just anything that interfered with "use of the public way." And the way kids spray the bullets at other kids, isn't that, in our time, the biggest interference in the public way? So maybe there isn't a case exactly like it in the England of Sir Edward Coke. But the England of Sir Edward Coke didn't hand out handguns to kids.

It's a big secret that the Right doesn't want people to know: it's not the Constitution, but the common law, where for ten centuries, there has been the most judicial activisim. Much of what is in Sir Edward Coke is his fantasy of what people were doing legally in the Middle Ages. It's a little like reading Tolkien.

But sometimes, under the common law, the courts do "make it up." But under the common law, it can be as much up to the judge as to the legislature, to stop something. There can be, and sometimes should be, two parallel systems of regulation.

So, yes, I'd love to file a case like this. But the moral, or ethical problem is: How can I, as a small-firm lawyer, ask somebody, like Soros, for a grant, when children are starving in Latin America, and a big firm could do the case much better anyway? Oh sure, I scoff at the big firms, and their pro bono. Don't the big-firm lawyers themselves joke about it?

In a big D.C. law firm, a friend of mine, O., told me of a firm meeting many years ago. As all the big business lawyers talked about the firm's pro bono, and asked, "What more should we be doing?," a young associate raised his hand.

"Given the work we normally do," he said, "if we really wanted to do something pro bono, maybe we should all just stay home from work for a single day."

But if the big firms can do a lot, by what moral right can I raise my hand and say, Give me money? None. It's too bad, but I should step aside. Years ago, I had a big case, to help clean up a union. But then the government came in. And one of the five Assistant U.S. Attorneys came over and said, in a nice way:

Thanks for calling us in. Now get out of the way. And the worst of it was—he was right! Now that the big boys were in, I ought to get out of the way.

But ah, I still want to do something in the world. But aside from the moral questions, etc., I've learned that, anyway, the foundations don't give grants for litigation. Or as a fundraiser told me: "You want a grant? I can get you a grant, sure. But I can't get you a grant to file a *suit!*"

"Why not?"

"Because the foundations won't do them. Not Soros. Not Ford." But if I want to get a grant for social change, I can get a grant, as a lawyer. The problem is, I'd have to lobby.

Now in the old days I thought you couldn't lobby. But thanks to the Christian Right, there have been changes in the IRS regulations, and now, it seems, on the Left as on the Right, everybody is a lobbyist.

So if I want to stop handguns, I have to lobby? I have to promise not to litigate? That's ridiculous. I wish I could explain to the foundations: When I'm filing a lawsuit, I *am* being a lobbyist. That's how, most of the time, private lawsuits lead to social change. Now I'd like to digress a bit and explain this. It's common now for professors to teach law students, Oh, the courts don't bring about social change. There is a well-known book on this: *The Hollow Hope,* by Gerald Rosenberg (1991). He debunks the idea that even in the civil rights era, the courts did much to bring about social change. After *Brown v. Board of Education* (1954) outlawed segregation in the schools, the schools in the

South became more segregated, legally, than before. So what ended segregation, the legal kind? Martin Luther King. The marches. It had nothing to do with Atticus Finch types, twittering like birds.

True? That lawyers like Thurgood Marshall were wasting their time?

Come on!

Read the book carefully. It turns out that ending Jim Crow did have a lot to do with courts. After King's marches, it was the Justice Department in the 1960s, going into court and filing suit after suit: that's what really desegregated the schools. So the Rosenberg school would say: But that's not the private Atticus Finch types, chirping for change?

Okay, but why did Justice file the suits? Sure, King's marches in the South. But what changed the climate, so King could march, and be so compelling, was the fact that *Brown v. Board was* the law. Yes, it's simplistic to say *Brown* by itself desegregated the schools. But *Brown* led to King. King led to Justice filing suit after suit.

In *The Hollow Hope,* a very intelligent man argues that you can't use the courts to change society, because society is just too set in its ways, too immovable. And what's his proof for his thesis, that society is unchangeable.

America in the 1960s. There you go. A decade when lawyers were rioting in the courts!

Of course you can change the world! It just doesn't happen in any direct or simplistic way. The other day I was thinking of this when I met a government lawyer on the subway:

"Hey Rob."

"Hi."

We know each other. He put down his paper. Somehow, looking at me, he began to talk about how private lawyers never accomplish anything. "I am fortunate," he said, "when I was in law school, I had

Archie Cox. . . ." (He means Cox, the Special Prosecutor, whom Nixon fired.) "Yeah, Archie used to laugh at these lawyers who want to use the courts like this, and he'd tell us, 'There's no group more timid than a bunch of federal judges . . . they're the last people who'd ever change the world.'"

Rob paused. "Of course Archie was an old New Dealer, and he said to us, if you want to change something, be a government lawyer."

Rob smiled. Since he was a government lawyer.

But how badly I wanted to say, at that moment: But see, Rob? Then all I have to do is lobby a government lawyer!

Brown v. Board was the best way to lobby them.

Anyway, I would have said this to Rob, but I figured that one day I may have to lobby him.

So that's how I have had what luck I've had. Usually I file the suit, and then the fact of the suit is a way to lobby the government lawyer. Or you use it as a way to bring pressure. It can be reform of the Teamsters. Or handguns.

And aside from all this, there is just out-and-out lobbying. Break up Microsoft? Lobby the Justice Department (Clinton's, anyway). Do something about tobacco? Bring enough suits, and the government will come in to file. It's astonishing to me that people actually doubt, yes, even in this conservative time, you can use the courts for social change! Of course you can use them for social change. That's what I'd try to tell kids now.

Even the little kids, the ones I tutored at the boys' home. One of them told me he wanted to be a lawyer, he was reading a book about it.

"What's the book?"

"Here." It was a book by John Gotti's lawyer, about his life with Gotti.

"You . . . This is awful, don't read this!" I shouted. And I threw the book down. Though it looked interesting.

"What should I read?"

"What about *To Kill a Mockingbird*?"

"What's that?"

So I told him about Atticus Finch, how you could go into little courtrooms, and, and . . . change the world!

It was weird how emotional I became about how this kid could just . . . well, go into court and change the world!

Later on I thought, I'll have to tell him about being a lobbyist. Anyway, the point is, you can use the courts for social change. That's not the problem. That's not what really galls me.

38. "YES, I ADMIT, I'D USE THE COURTS FOR SOCIAL CHANGE!"

What galls me now is that, at least in our time, I can't use them for equality. Save the whales. Save the oceans. Save Rolando, even. Or save some poor wretch from going to the chair. Yes, maybe that. But I can't use them to raise wages. To close the gap between rich and poor.

I can't use them for equality, which is why I went to law school. So if that's what I want, what's the point of being a lawyer?

I know that even to say this makes some people gasp. How dare you, etc. But when I went to law school in the 1960s, equality was hot. Since the New Deal, year after year, the passion for it had been building. I could show in a graph how incomes were coming closer together. And what I'd love to tell a law school class, in Nome or El Paso, is the strange thing that Montesquieu points out: how the more equality there is, the more people want it. Indeed, at one time, this passion, or love of equality, is the very thing that made America so different from Europe. Now, it's our love of *inequality* that makes America . . . well, so different from Europe. But talk to people on the street, and many will say, "But it's always been that way." That's what's so 1984ish. People don't remember. But my problem is, I can't forget the way people talked when I was Rolando's age, twenty-two. We didn't even think about things like capital punishment. It didn't exist. Nor did prison. All people talked about in law school was, as I fancifully recall, civil rights, the Warren Court, the Fourteenth Amendment, locking up the principle of equality in the Constitution.

The 1960s were strange, but we'd had other ages like this before. The Age of Jackson. The Age of Lincoln. And while we seemed to lose the passion for equality after the Civil War, it came back again, first with the Progressives, then with the New Dealers, then with the Great Society. And in the law schools, I can carve it up into eras:

First, the age of corporate law: 1900–1920. Louis Brandeis. Trust-busting. Break up Standard Oil, more or less as with Microsoft.

Then the age of labor law: 1930–1954. The New Deal, the Wagner Act. The hot law for the young hotshot GIs coming back from the war. Robert Kennedy, in a way, was a labor lawyer. It was the rage.

Then the age of constitutional law: 1954–1974. Lock it up in the Constitution. Use the Equal Protection clause of the Fourteenth Amendment. Civil rights for blacks. Then economic rights for everyone. The big case in my time in law school, or so I would say, is not *Roe v. Wade* but the now forgotten *San Antonio Ind. School District v. Rodriguez* (1973). In that case, lawyers argued that the Fourteenth Amendment prohibited unequal funding of the public schools.

Imagine, that was the issue. Did the Constitution prohibit an inequality based on wealth, income!

Ah, if only *Rodriguez* had gone the other way! I didn't know it, but that was the case in which, as a culture of lawyers, we made the U-turn. Our Thermidor.

• • •

So we only lost 5 to 4. And who'd have thought after this, inequality would explode? Anyway, because there were such cases, back then, "that's why you went to law school." And I'm not ashamed to say it now.

It seems weird, though. In a democracy, is this any way to march to equality, i.e., go into law, come out on my knees, to beg a judge?

Why not use majority rule? That's what people say when they scoff: Use the majoritarian process. Don't try this elite route to social change.

Now what's my answer? I have none. If I must choose between majority rule and judicial activism, I'll stammer, and I'd say it's a false choice, etc. But I suppose if I'm really pressed, I'd have to clear my throat and say, Well, yes, I'm for majority rule.

The problem is, there is no *national* majority rule. That's not a rhetorical point. It's the way the Constitution is set up. As few as forty senators representing nine . . . as in 9, NINE . . . percent of the population can block any bill. Thus it is impossible to use majority rule to pass a bill giving people the right to join a union, or any other right.

And precisely because there is no *national* majority rule, both Right and Left use the courts. For different reasons. In the case of the Left, because there isn't majority rule, or a system of government based on one person, one vote. In the case of the Right, it's to stop unions, mangle labor laws . . . so we don't end up with what majority rule produces.

Up until the 1930s, we know that courts were knocking down state laws on hours, wages, to help the majority. And of course they enjoined people from going on strike at all. So inequality grew.

But after the New Deal? Much the same as far as strikes go, but more subtle. Yes, even the sainted Warren Court did as much as it could to stop working people from going on strike. Unions became weaker.

Sometimes it was in the guise of doing good: i.e., to have arbitrations instead of a strike. But the point is that courts in America hate the "disorder" of a strike. That's their role in American history. Stop the strike. Or even the threat of a strike. It's hard to overstate the fact that in every other country it's different. In Britain, France, etc., *courts don't do this.* In America, and only in America, activist courts stop people from striking, and in the end, of course, from having any effective unions at all.

Yet it's not so simple, because at times courts have been a force for equality. For the same reason that they're a force for *in*equality: because we don't have true or pure majority rule. But I'd just as soon do it the European way: straight-out majority rule.

But if the other side, business, etc., is using the courts for their social change, I might as well use it for mine as well. What choice do I have? Because in an ultimate sense, the courts determine in large part how income is distributed.

And that determines how many people are in prison. Or so argue the sociologists I read in *Scientific American*. So in this odd way, what I and others do as civil lawyers determine how many young persons should be criminal lawyers like Scott.

So yes, I'd use the courts for social change, for more equality, if I could get away with it. The problem at the moment is: I can't. Besides, the way the practice of law is set up now, I can't even get equality for me.

39. THAT'S THE *MEDIAN?*

Yes, how can lawyers, today, bring equality to the country? We can't even bring it to ourselves. The other day I was having lunch with my friend Richard. He's one of those solo lawyers with a firm name of Richard ———— and Associates, which means him and a group of kids, law students who have access to free Lexis and Westlaw.

"Still hate being a lawyer?"

For some reason, people keep asking me this.

"You know, for a lawyer, what the median is, in Illinois?"

"No." I hoped he wouldn't tell me.

"It's fifty thousand," said Richard.

"Dollars?" I was coughing.

"Yeah, fifty thousand dollars . . . that's the median."

"No," I said. "No! You're sure?"

He nodded and went on: "For a while I was making no money. Now I'm making some. Some."

"Yeah, I'm . . . I'm making some." (But I was thinking, that's the *median?*)

"And the really crazy thing is, I work hard. . . ."

I nodded, I do too. But how could that be the median, which half of us are *under?*

Anyway, a few days later I went to lunch to raise money for lawyers in Legal Services. And the speaker was droning, "We all know what a sacrifice these lawyers make, many of them make only seventy thousand dollars . . . blah, blah. . . ."

I whispered to Bob, "You know what? Lawyers for the poor, they actually raise the median."

"What do you mean?" Bob whispered back.

"I mean, I heard the other day . . . the median is fifty thousand dollars."

"No," said Bob. "That's impossible!"

"Shhh. . . . I'm telling you. . . ."

But then I decided: better find out. It turns out that lawyers for the poor are actually at the median. Or at least Professor John Heinz has a study that for lawyers in Chicago, the Loop, with the big law firms, the overall median (1995) was close to eighty-five thousand dollars. It would be much lower if the suburbs, or especially the whole state were included, though he did not include them in his study. It was Professor Heinz who told me of Sherwin Rosen's book, *Winner Take All* (1991).

In *Winner Take All,* Rosen, an economist, shows that lawyers at the top, in the big firms, take all the money. From lawyers at the bottom. Even lawyers in the middle, like Richard ———— and Associates. In a way, this is a model for what happened to the country in the 1990s. The inequality grew not between high school v. college but between college v. college. Even within the same college. Even within the same law school. I know.

It happened to law, to most lawyers. It happened to doctors: that's why some unionized. It happened to engineers. In general, if you were in a learned profession in the 1990s, you probably took a hit, because of what Rosen calls Winner Take All.

So now in the oldest, most learned professions, which go back to the Middle Ages, the way the money is divided up lately makes the least sense of all.

But how can that be? Are the lawyers in the top firms so much better? To the contrary. They *should* be better. The brightest kids in the class go there, etc., but they don't go to trial, etc., yes, even less than the rest of us. So up there it takes a long, long time to get any training. And look at Richard, who can do a divorce, then draft a will, or take an immigration case. No one in the big firms can do this. Dementia starts early up there. They do the same things over and over again. Except for the hours, the work itself, at the top, has less variety. It's not as hard. Even among the big firms there is at least an urban legend thing that Chicago big-firm lawyers are better litigators than New York lawyers, even though New York lawyers get more money. I hope I'm being objective when I say that if I picked out lawyers to represent me, and money were no object, I wouldn't go anywhere near the big firms. I'm up against these lawyers, and they're not the ones who scare me.

So it's not survival of the fittest. In Darwinian terms it's not really natural selection. It's more like "sexual selection." Peahens are attracted to the peacocks with the biggest tails, even though they're the very ones that are the clumsiest, the least nimble, etc. In the same way, the bigger your income, the bigger your tail. And the more certain types of clients are attracted to you. Few of these guys would survive against Scott at Twenty-sixth and Cal. But the bigger their tails, the more the clients go into heat.

So it's easy to explain Winner Takes All. The puzzle is why Richard and me and the lawyers who'd make more money being lawyers for the poor, keep on whacking away at it. But I know what the appeal is for me:

The job is impossible.

It's so impossible, it's hypnotic. As a small-firm lawyer I have to fill out, lick my pencil even, a little time sheet every day. Maybe put in six entries. But really, if I had the time to think them all out, I might end up with sixteen. The other night I had dinner with a woman who asked, "What did you do today?" She's a scientist and studies human behavior, so this was a deadly serious question. *What did you do today?*

Well . . . I started in probate. That had been weird, so I especially remembered it. "Oh," said a lawyer I saw up there, "what are *you* doing up here, on the 'money floor'?"

Yes, it was for a guy with twenty-seven children. A lot of unknown heirs.

Then back to the office. Union health insurance . . . just cut off. Emergency. Then . . . oh, I listed six or seven items for her.

"Oh, I wrote a letter to a lawyer next."

And all through dinner, I'd pipe up: "Oh, and I just remembered something else. . . ."

Later: "Oh, and another thing . . ."

Later, at dessert: "My God, I forgot, *I was spending all afternoon writing a brief!*"

And that's why I do it. I'm fascinated by how many plates are in the air. Fascinated. All day I look up, childlike, at all the plates. They don't have to *pay* me.

And if that sounds like some weird taste of mine, I think it's true even at the top of our profession. Remember, thanks to Clinton, the taxes on the Big Firm Partners, i.e., the people at the top, went up in the 1990s. Now in economic logic, this means that people should have cut back the extra work "at the margin." Why spend that extra hour at the office? But if anything, raising taxes on people at the top seemed to make them work even harder.

So we raised taxes on the rich. And inequality grew. CEO incomes got bigger. So there's a lesson for the Right. But I'd say there's also a lesson for the Left: Using the tax rate to reduce inequality doesn't really work. What works is giving power to the people at the bottom . . . maids, factory workers, lawyers like me . . . to get a bigger share through unions, collective bargaining. That's what will stop Winner Take All.

But there's yet another lesson: that our best educated would flock to a job where they get a toilet income. And stay. Year after year!

If that's true, then maybe we don't need any large gap in income to get people to work incredible hours. In a certain sense, it doesn't matter how much money people are making at Kirkland and Ellis. I'm not bothered.

I'll still practice anyway.

It's just what they're making that first year at Kirkland and Ellis.

40. LEVITATION

I've always wanted to know why I can't be a first-year associate. *Right now.* They can't have an age limit, can they? Yes, it would be demeaning. A little. But remember . . . at Sullivan, at other firms, some of the kids are making:

> . . . *$165,000 a year.*

And up.

How often when the Big Firm Partner wants to settle and says, "We'll take care of your legal fees," I want to say: No. Not my fees . . . if you really want to settle this, *take me on as a first-year associate.*

Then after a year I could go on to Twenty-sixth and Cal. As did Scott, though Scott was in his twenties when he left the big firm. Could I do it at age fifty? Not that I doubt my skill. As my friend Richard said at lunch, "Remember how it used to take us two weeks to draft a complaint?"

"Or two months," I said.

"Now we can do it in a day."

I thought how in a few pro bono cases, I have worked with kids from big corporate firms. And when they show me their "complaints," like little drawings, I laugh, but it's scary to think, This kid is making $165,000 as a first-year?

Actually, I see them only in the fourth year. It's often, when I'm opposing counsel, at the very start of a case: "the kid" is the lawyer. It's a tactic of the Big Partner to stay in his captain's quarters at first. And so for the first six months or so of a Title VII sex discrimination case, I only see one of the midshipmen, usually it's a "Kimberly." This is to let me know my place: The captain can't be bothered.

Then, about a year or so into the case, the captain comes out of his quarters, since he's now made his point: This case is beneath me, etc., and soon enough, that's all over, and the two of us snap at each other, and it's as if "Kimberly" were never there. And by the way, what did they do with her? Did she leave the firm? Two years after the filing, no sign of her. It'd be a good question for an interrogatory:

Q: Where's Kimberly?

But it'd be treated like every other interrogatory under the Rules, and they wouldn't answer. And of course, to my shame, the tactic does work. I yell at Kimberly. If she tries to say something, I interrupt her. It may seem sexist, because why am I feminizing it, and talking about "Kimberly" when it could just as well be a "Brad"? For two reasons. First, I never see a "Brad." I think that in the big firms they have a feeling that, with me at least, they should first send out a "Kimberly" for the first six months. As Tom F. says, "When it's women, you can't yell at them, they take it so personally." So then why do I take it so personally? I go home and brood: When have I let Kimberly finish a sentence?

Second, they probably do send out "Brads." I just don't remember any.

I said this to another friend, Jim, and he shrugged. "What could be less interesting than sitting down, having a 'conversation' with a young person, that age, you know . . . who's a *guy?*" But there's a dark reason, too, for my interest in the "Kimberlys," and it's partly because I hate these firms so much. Yes, it's true, it is Winner Take All. And I'll admit, in part anyway, it is a kind of class war. They may have all the money, a starting salary of $165,000, so it's easy to start thinking, Yeah, I can take these guys, make their lives hell. I can blow up their supply lines. Take the cologne from the firm bathroom. . . . But I think if I were honest, I'd realize that what I want is the revenge, the ultimate, that of the criollo class against the Spanish who came over to rule, and what is that revenge, the ultimate that we could inflict on the big firm? *Steal their women.*

But it would be wrong. And when I did think about it (was it over twenty years ago? Good God), I didn't have the nerve. What would I have said on the date? I mean, she's making over $165,000 a year! *Where do you take her?* "I've got an idea? Let's pretend tonight we're graduate students, and sit way, way up in the upper balcony, and . . . ?"

That's one date.

Anyway, though there is a kind of war, you never—or I would never—take it that far. It did cross my mind once, but that was all.

The firm bathroom, that's different. I remember the day I really came to hate, really *hate,* Kirkland and Ellis. It was before faxes, and I was late filing a brief, so I walked the damn thing over, and was sweating. And like a messenger, a UPS guy with a tie, I asked the receptionist, "You mind if I use the bathroom?"

"No."

"No?"

"It's only for members of the firm." She couldn't be bothered even to look at me.

I bit my lip. Should I leave? I said, "Could you call Mr. Newton?" (Now, Mr. Newton was a god, a senior partner.) She stared. "I said, could you tell Mr. Newton to come down here to the lobby? He's my opposing counsel. And just say that I want him to come down here to take me to the bathroom."

She stared.

"Go ahead," I said. "PICK UP THE PHONE." (I was out of control, I'm ashamed to say.)

She picked the phone up, I'll say that, and she even started to dial . . . then she put it down. "Go ahead."

"What? I didn't hear you."

"I said," she said, "go *ahead!*" She pointed with her arm. "Go ahead! You can use the bathroom!" It's like the way they give up their documents when you drag them into court.

·   ·   ·

And am I jealous? Because one year as an associate in these places, and I'd be . . . well, *am* I jealous? I don't know! Most of the time, and this sounds strange to say, I feel sorry that these kids are making so much money. The other day a friend of mine in a big firm . . . and yes, I have a few . . . he was saying at lunch, "The starting salary, what we pay now, you know what it is?"

"No."

"I hate to tell you," he said.

"Go ahead." (It's odd, I don't mind hearing, it doesn't have much effect on me.)

When he told me, I fainted. But later I remember a new associate who complained to me how she was making too much money.

"They offered me another raise! Oh, I don't want it."

She sighed. "I feel sorry for the younger ones coming in. . . ." She sighed again. "Do you know what I mean? It just leads to . . ."

She trailed off.

I took a guess. "Disorder?"

"Disorder. That's it. Disorder." Isn't she right? The big firms are like pushers. In my mind I can see an ad, on the El, for young people

First photo: *"This is your brain in law school."* Gray, normal.

Second: *"This is your brain on $165,000 a year."* It's orange. Or fire.

Now, against myself, I'd like to suggest that the more you pay the kids, the more, paradoxically, they really are "worth the money." I know I compared the big-firm lawyers to peacocks, but still the peacocks get into nasty fights with each other. Any law, even peacock law, is all about willpower, who can stay up the latest (see Clausewitz, *On War*) and at $165,000 a year, some kids not only "stay up," they levitate. It's like a high from the money, like the drug Ecstasy, which, in the clubs, so I hear, the young now lick off each other's arms. If I were a Big Firm Partner, I'd be glad for my own sake to pay a kid that much o more. Then he or she would stay up all night, spontaneously combust even, be like a firewall between me and all the big-firm peacocks on the other side.

Sometimes when I have seen a young associate in her cubicle, it's as if she, too, is in a certain light. Yes, sort of like . . . Twenty-sixth and Cal. At least I feel the same creepy way I did when I saw the holding cell and thought, Get this kid out of here!

It's odd that at $165,000 a year, the kids seem to need a union. If they only made *less,* they'd have a higher standard of living. Why? Because it's not human to live like this. There's no dignity.

Even at the top, in this country, we could use a little human rights. A woman lawyer I know told me of a pal who went, at twenty-six, into a big firm. "I'm thirty-nine," he said, "but Theresa, I have no memory of the last thirteen years." No memory. His life, gone.

That's why even at eleven o'clock at night when I'm too exhausted to see, I try to read one or two pages of, oh, Churchill, just so I can say, Well, today at least I lived! (for a few minutes). And my hero at doing this is J. Once, at the Wall Street Deli on Monday afternoon, I found him, woozy, stumbling. "My wife and I," he said, "we took Friday off and flew to Istanbul." Istanbul, for the weekend! The food on the plane back had made him sick. He'd rushed back to do a brief. But at least for a weekend he had lived!

But what of the young women who, like Sister Carrie, come to Chicago and go to work in the big firms? Some never get out. They get addicted. But others do. I somehow believe that a young woman like this has to check into a hotel, shut the door . . . and for a month or so go into withdrawal. That's how she gets off the $165,000 a year.

I saw one back out on the street the other day. Once, she was in a big firm that let her go. But I knew this even before she told me. She had a washed-out-but-I'm-better sort of look. How to put this?

Maybe . . . she had lost her "powers." She can't levitate anymore. She's fallen back to earth. Now she's one of us.

You even think, you could marry her now. But after the Ecstasy, the levitating . . . well, you have to wonder what the baby would look like.

Anyway, now I've given up the idea of being first-year. For at my age, I can't levitate. I'm not "combustible," the way I was when I was younger. I'm too old to "catch fire" in the way a Big Firm Partner has a right to expect. Besides, my being there would demoralize the kids. After a certain age as a lawyer, you give off a smell of failure.

But after years of glancing at letters from big firms threatening motions to compel, etc., I've come up with an idea for getting out of law. By chance one day I began to read, truly read, the names of the cities of the branch offices that they now list on the letterhead. Whether it's Sidley and Austin or Baker and MacKenzie, there is now a list like:

London
Paris
Vilnius

Now, I've no chance to land a London or Paris, but how about Vilnius, or Minsk? Why not let me go out to relieve the guy way out there in Tashkent? I'll go, I'm not married.

For a long time I didn't believe that Firm "X" here had a lawyer out in Vilnius or Minsk. But at a Christmas party for the firm, a paralegal there I know said, "He's here tonight, want to meet him?"

Actually he'd been out there and was back. At the party he didn't want to talk about it.

"Let's just say I'm glad I'm back here."

What I'd love to know is what the big firms pay to send a lawyer.

solo, way out there on the steppes. Could it be, do you think, $165,000 a year? The place I have in mind to go is . . . Tashkent. I met a Russian who did his army service there, and he says, "Tashkent is lovely, it's very green."

Sure, I'd miss my friends, the public-interest types, the labor lawyers. But at least out in Tashkent there would be a whole new legal system.

As the only big-firm lawyer out there, I'm sure I'd get to like Winner Take All.

41. INEQUALITY IS ALL THE RAGE

I've wondered: Why does the fighting between lawyers seem to get worse and worse? I believe it has something to do with the fact that our clients have fewer rights.

Now I know the Right beats into us: "Oh Americans, we're too rights-oriented." Except of course when it comes to guns. And it's true there is a whole system of civil rights laws. Rights to be free from discrimination based on age, race, sex, handicap.

But the result is, as a friend says: "In this country you can't be fired for age, race, sex, handicap, blah, blah . . . except of course, that you can be fired for any reason at any time."

So if other people aren't as rights-oriented, it's because they can be fired only for just cause. While in this country, the more rights our clients have, the more impotent they are. So all we can do is file lawsuits that we can't really win . . . and scream.

And the maddening thing is, while the bosses and the rich complain about all these employment cases, it's the bosses and the rich who are the most effective in using these laws as *plaintiffs*. Who gets the golden parachute? The guy with the most money to hire the

Big Dog, lawyer-wise. As every company knows, it's the fired vice president you want to buy off. Thanks to depositions, production of documents, it's a plaintiff like this who can cause you the most damage.

So the civil rights laws that Martin Luther King marched for? I'm afraid even these work mainly for the rich.

So why do the rich complain? It's an odd thing about Winner Take All, that even people at the top are screaming too. Every year, even at the top, in the Big Firms, the lawyers up there seem more and more pissed off.

Especially in discovery. It amazes me. Why in the big firms do they refuse to produce documents? Yes, yes, I know why, it's the game, etc. And yet I really don't know why. Who cares, really? The other day S. (another S.) was telling me at lunch about a guy our age who was fighting with a young lawyer, maybe thirty. "The guy suddenly thought, Wait, I'm over fifty. I don't give a shit, do I? I mean, my life is over. So he turned to the kid and said, 'Hey, you want this document? Fine. It's yours.' The kid says, 'What?' The guy says, 'It's yours. All of them. Anything you want.' "

I nodded, knowing what this meant: In the tribe of lawyers, it means the poor guy had decided to lie down and die.

But sometimes the lawyer who wins is the lawyer who fights the least.

I remember how I had to shout at a client the other day. We were about to file our case, and he started jumping up and down: "Ah, this is war! This is war!"

"No!" I said. "Calm down. This isn't 'war.' "

"Wait, but aren't we going to kick a little ass?"

"No. No, we aren't going to 'kick a little ass.' " I told him that a lawyer can't think like that. The judges hate all the fighting. In a way, the legal profession is a trap: It draws in the really testy kids, who like to argue, and then later they go to court, and there's no trial, and the judge just keeps groaning, "Can't you people agree on anything?"

So of late, this is my rule: that sometimes in a court, the best thing is just say nothing.

I know a lawyer who's superb at this. He is a very, very big man, who could hold his own in a bar. Yet at a status, while other lawyers rant and call names, it often seems at first he is going to say nothing.

And everyone gets edgy. And yells louder. And even the judge starts to look over. Now, that's very good: Get the judge to come to you. Make the judge beg for it.

Then, then he talks. But even then he pitches his voice so that people lean over slightly . . . and then:

BAM.

He crushes them. But it's soft, too. It's only later, at home at night, you punch your fist through some boards.

Anyway, imagine: Winner Take All, and everyone feeling cheated. And no one, ever, can blow it off in a trial. Let me tell you how nasty it can get. I mentioned the suit in public nuisance against manufacturers of handguns. One day I got a phone call: "Would you attend a debate about this case in front of our organization . . . the Federalist Society?"

He was a young lawyer, quite polite. And I have to admit, it would be a big dinner, and very civic-minded, and I was flattered to be asked. So I of course gave the only answer I could:

No.

No way. Absolutely not. The Federalist Society? The guys who run around in wigs? No, no, no. . . .

But then my co-counsel accepted, so that was the end of that. Now, my co-counsel is a real trial lawyer, and knows far more about the case. So I was along for the ride, again, sort of second chair, if that. And when we arrived at the restaurant, I began to think, How bad can this be? I saw lawyers even from the big firms.

It's true, I noticed the lawyers were drinking.

Anyway my co-counsel went first. Calm. Rational. How the law of public nuisance applied, etc. Sir Edward Coke, and so on. Then in the back, a lawyer began to yell, "Wait, hey, didn't this guy defend a Cop Killer?!

"Yeah, you! Didn't you defend a COP killer??"

And then came a snarling, maybe a hundred lawyers out there, but it was something I'd not heard even on talk radio. I even saw someone mouth, Fuck you.

Then someone was not mouthing, but saying, "Fuck you!"

Later I wondered if two or only one had said it? My co-counsel didn't hear it. But the thing that struck me was: With all the money they make, why be in such a rage?

Perhaps a few of the big-firm lawyers there were jealous of my co-counsel, who actually tries cases. Meanwhile, *they* know they haven't been to trial for years. Anyway, I can swear from personal experience, a hostile mob of Teamsters would be more polite.

At the end, in fairness, I must say that the young lawyer who was president of the Federalists came over to apologize. Touched, I wanted to say to the kid, You're too nice to be part of this.

But of course, I could say that of the profession. It's Winner Take All. Inequality is all the rage.

42. THE PROBLEM IS, IT'S ALL THE WHEEL

The one trouble I have in recommending law school is that the Legal System We Now Have may be no system at all. Equal Protection, Due Process—what do either of them mean? Go ahead, file a suit. Maybe you will change the world. Only the problem is, more than ever:

It's All the Wheel.

And what is the Wheel? The Wheel is a stack of stickers with the names of judges, and when you file a case the first time up on the twentieth floor in federal court here, the clerk peels off a sticker . . . and slap, there's the judge. You can get any one of thirty judges. A name is peeled, no order. It can be: "Smith, Smith, Smith," six times in a row, then no "Smith" for six weeks. Why? Forget it. Go home. Remember. It's all the Wheel.

And the Wheel is the Law, and the Law is the Wheel. And really, that is my life, or one's life as a civil lawyer. Of the thirty judges over at 219 South Dearborn, two or so are so deadly to me that if I were to draw them on a case they really took a hating to, then for years to come I'd be haunted by more demons and voices than a grad student in Russia.

By wild luck, this has yet to happen to me. But as I write this, I think of a friend of mine who is a "dead man walking," and the reason is . . . it's All the Wheel.

In the old days, I understand, you could rig the Wheel. And that's one of the secrets behind how, once upon a time in the South, a lawyer could use the law for social change. In the 1950s and 1960s, in Montgomery, Alabama, in the time of George Wallace, there were only two judges sitting. One, Frank Johnson, would whack down every form of apartheid or segregation, while the other judge wouldn't matter. Now, the names of the two judges came off the Wheel in perfect order: Johnson, Judge X., Johnson, Judge X. . . . So if you had a really Big Case, you just held it till you had two Little Ones to file as well. Now, if you filed the first Little One and it went to Judge X., then you handed up the Big Case as your next. But if the first Little One went to Johnson, you held the Big Case to the end. By the time someone in the clerk's office could stop this, the Rule of Law, unfairly, had come to Alabama.

Now it's all the Wheel down there the way it is up here.

•   •   •

I'm terrified to go over, in person, to file. I . . . can't watch them peel the label. I shake. That's why I send Phyllis, our secretary, who's very ethereal, plays the viola. She goes over, humming. Files. Comes back to the office. Smiles at me. Sits down to work again.

"Oh, Phyllis," I say. I come out of my office.

"Hmm?" she says, humming.

"You . . . you filed the complaint?"

Smiles. "Oh, yes."

She goes back to work, hums.

"Phyllis . . . who did we get?"

"Hmm?"

"What judge? *Who is it?*"

She looks at me. "Oh." She picks up a complaint and reads it:

"Randleton." (I've made up this name.)

Randleton?

A half minute goes by. "Huh. Well," I say. "Randleton is . . . is . . . not bad."

A whole minute. "Randleton . . . actually is good."

Two minutes. "Oh, my God, Randleton is great!" Now I run into the office of my wonderful partner, Len, and I'm waving my arms: "WE GOT RANDLETON!"

"Oh, that's good!" he says.

"GOOD?" I shout. "RANDLETON IS *GREAT!!*" Because now I know that in at least one more case I-will-not-be-disbarred. In two years we'll settle. How strange that in those two years I may never *see* Randleton, except for two or three minutes at a status. On the street if one day I ever pass him, he'll nod, but think, Who is that? So why is Randleton so important? Because we need him to: (1) certify the class; or (2) deny a motion to dismiss. One or other. Then, as lawyers, we can go ahead and settle the case without him. Litigation is like a huge game of rotisserie baseball, and in many a case (not all, but many) we can go on and "play," even though our real-life judge is mostly off the field. It's mysterious even to me, after all my years at law, why the sticker peeled off and slapped on the complaint matters *that* much. Isn't there "the law"? Yes, of course, there's "law." So would he not follow—? No, no. The opposite. He's very careful. Cautious. All the Clinton judges are. Then how is Randleton—? I can't explain. It's just—they control our world in ways that are very hard to see. It's like the heavens when I look up at night. What I see with my eye is everything that burns, gives off light, but the lighted part is small, and most of the stuff that's up there is what we call black holes. And the big cases decided by the appellate courts are like the suns and the stars. But more than nine tenths of all cases orbit way off, in the dark, around the black holes, to which I'd compare the different district judges, or their courtrooms, into which, without giving off light, our cases disappear.

To me the black holes are vastly more important than the sun and stars. By that I mean, I would gladly, or with a gulp or two, accept that up on the Supreme Court there be nine Clarence Thomases, or nine Antonin Scalias. All I ask is that I get to appoint the lower bench, every single one of the district judges.

Because in real life, I will never see a Thomas or a Scalia, I hope (or otherwise I wouldn't write this), but down below in the boiler room, this is where I'm settling the cases. In *The Common Law* (1892), the great Holmes made his cynical *bon mot:* Law is nothing more than "predicting what judges do."

But how do you predict which judge you're going to get? (It doesn't matter what they "do." As I said, the judge may only vaguely know I have a case before him.)

Let me tell of two judges, "U." and "Y." The one who is "U."—and this is one of the guys who make it feel like "Russia"—is on the

Right. Is he as slow-witted as some disgruntled lawyers say or insecure—or is he mean?

In fact, deep down, I think he's a nice guy. I may be one of the few lawyers (on the Left) over there who do. Still, I admit, if a judge really is both incompetent *and* scared, then I like to see them a little higher up, like up on the Supreme Court. Maybe the Court of Appeals. The problem is when they get a serious job: sitting as a district judge. After all these years, Judge U. still has yet to figure out how to relax at a status.

Simple status. Our case is one of twenty. Judge U. begins: "Gentlemen."

(It's like we're all from the Yale Club.)

"Ahem. Gentlemen. What brings you before The Court?"

("The Court?" It's only him!)

"Uh, Judge, we're here on a status." (What does he think? Now *all* of us are getting nervous.)

Then I sometimes think of my first pretrial before him. Yes, a while ago, it was my first time before Judge U., back in his chambers. When I and opposing counsel came in, we saw he had been going through the file.

"Well, gentlemen. The Court has been reviewing this case. And let me say, The Court can see where this is heading. Oh yes, The Court can see right now what is going to happen if this goes to trial."

He paused. Then he pointed at me: "You! Your witnesses, they're all going to come in here and say one thing." Then he turned to my opponent: "And you, Mr. ———! Your witnesses, they're all going to come in here and say just the opposite."

"So?" he paused. *"How am I supposed to decide?"*

Well, that was certainly going to be a problem. Or it would be if he ever tried a civil case, which I don't believe he has. What happened to our case?

Dismissed. I forget the reason the law clerk came up with. The real reason of course was that the witnesses were going to say different things. Or: *Dismissed, parties refuse to settle.*

Then just for contrast, I'll mention going for a settlement with Judge Y. As a magistrate judge, she has to do what the official tenured-for-life judges give her to do, and that means: settle cases. I saw her on a Title VII sex discrimination case for two Hispanic women: two waitresses, who had fought to be promoted to doing "banquets" at a big downtown hotel. As waitresses on "extra" or on "standby" duty, they earned about fifteen thousand dollars. If the hotel would promote them to do banquets, the money would jump to eighty thousand dollars.

Yes: if these hotels ever let Hispanic women do the banquets.

But I want to tell you about Judge Y., and while her big job is to set bail and process criminals, there is a way, when I walked into her chambers, that she made me, and the two women, feel as if we'd come for tea. Oh, her *smile!*

"Oh," she said, "you know, settling cases, this is the part of my job I find the most fulfilling." She smiled. And from here on, she stopped looking at me and now stared at the two women.

"You know," said the Judge, "I'm just appointed to the bench. And I enjoy it very much. And while I like dealing with the lawyers . . ."—and here the Judge really nodded as if I might be in the room—". . . oh, I tell people, 'Oh! How I miss my clients!' "

My clients were smiling now. I liked the way this all was going.

"Your case," she said, "it's one we see a lot of. Did you know that over here in federal court, forty percent of our cases are employment cases now?"

No. We didn't.

And then she talked to the women about settling. "I have noticed something about the cases I settle here," she said. "No one who settles walks out happy. No one. And if we settle, you won't be either."

She let that take hold. And now the Judge said to them, "But so often, oh it may be three or four weeks later, the parties . . . yes, they phone me up, and they're happy now. And they say, 'Oh, Judge, we're so glad now that we settled!' "

And she sent us out and then talked to the Hotel. And when she called us back in, everyone was smiling. "You would never believe it," she said. "I wouldn't have believed it. But they're going to offer you jobs . . . as banquet servers!"

And we even got some back pay. And one of my clients was thrilled. And if the other was less so, she also finally went along. And if we did not all begin to cry, I at least was a little shaky. "Oh," I kept saying to the second woman, "now your children can go to college!" Why I kept saying this, two or three times, I just don't know. She must have thought, What is this?

So at moments, yes, there is the Rule of Law. Or is it just the Wheel? Judge U. and Judge Y. are about as different as Chad and Canada. It makes me wonder that in law school, along with or even instead of "Torts" or "Contracts," shouldn't we teach, say, just for example, "The Law of White Male Reagan Judges," and "The Law of Women Democrats Who Had Their Own Solo Practice"? But what I'd really like to teach right now is: "The Wheel." Since right now look at the mix of Clinton and Bush and Reagan judges whose names the clerks are peeling in the Northern District of Illinois, my home court:

Carter	2
Reagan	2
Bush Sr.	4
Clinton	13

Out of this can come only the jurisprudence of "Fortuna." And for a lawyer the sad thing is, to paraphrase Machiavelli, *The Prince,* "One can do everything right, be nice, be a jerk, at just the right times, and still you can come to naught." It *is* all the Wheel.

For a while, at the turn of this century, I was thinking, What an exciting time to be a lawyer. Because anything could happen. Sometimes I was up. Sometimes I was down. Oh sure, I was down whenever I saw some case that would make a judge immortal, or even save the city, and because of the Wheel, it would end up with Judge U. Ugh. And all this while some fresh young Clinton appointee, bright the way most of them were so bright, would end up with a—

Let's take Judge X.X. White male. So I asked a friend, "White guy, how'd he get it? Big firm?"

"No."

"Political connection?" I asked.

"No," said my friend. "I don't think so."

What's that leave? "Was . . . was it just merit?"

My friend was silent. "I don't know, I can't . . . what, wh–what else . . . would it be?"

Intelligence?

It's a strange and little-written thing about appointees of Clinton—not just judicial appointees, but all kinds: how bright they were. For Reagan, Bush Sr., Clinton, I'd like to have the percentage of Clinton judges who made it onto law review.

Now, supposedly, the Democrats have to be more "p.c." and "diverse." But the Republicans have a much bigger problem, to pick people who want to *overturn Roe v. Wade.* Among the crowd that would actually overturn it even now, there simply aren't enough minimally intelligent people to run a court. By contrast, look at Clinton: He could pick anybody. Some may say that the Republicans have another handicap, that *their* big-firm-lawyer types would have to take such pay cuts. But that's nonsense. Even in big firms, there are enough desperate people to fill these jobs. They're just not enough competent ones who are sufficiently wacky to be way out on the Far Right.

•   •   •

Beyond the Wheel and its turnings, somehow I *knew*, by that last year of Clinton, that the law was meekly changing. Look at all the Clinton appointees in that wonderful chart above. It was as if under these Clinton judges, whose names we don't even know, all the settlements that make up the dark matter of law were different, and creating a new, lighter mood in the country. I felt the law was becoming . . . nicer. But more than that, I felt that I could become nicer, too.

Maybe I could be a lawyer without being such a jerk at times. I think about how often I'm seething at a judge like Judge U. In the Gospel, Jesus says that you can be a murderer just by calling someone a fool. Judge U. has hurt a lot of people, in my view, but I don't think the man's a fool.

I don't want to overstate this (I already have), but I sensed that with the many new women judges, the many Clinton appointees, the law was moving mysteriously in some new direction. Something was going to be revealed, something big. But in a little way. Whatever was coming would not be like the 1960s this time, or like the Warren Court.

Just a new feeling. The settlements. The women judges.

Again, here's another number or statistic that I wish it were possible to know: for men and women judges as groups, the percentage of their settlements that do some good in the world.

I looked around in my own practice. I wasn't miserable anymore. How of late could I have drawn so many women judges on the Wheel?

To the extent that it gives me women or Clinton judges, the Wheel has been okay to me of late. Even when they're on the Right, and against, at least the women are less likely to ridicule the lawyers. I think here of a passage in *The Spirit of the Laws,* where Montesquieu is giving his ideal of the Prince. One quality, he says, is: *The Prince does not insult.* That's much truer of women judges. How nice to know: if I lose, at least I won't be insulted.

And the Prince does not threaten; the Prince allows the law to threaten. That is more true of women judges as well.

So yes, that year it felt more like the Wheel, and less like the Rule of Law. Holmes said the law is predicting what judges do because the judges back in his day were all the same. White and male and on the Right, smashing unions. It was the juries that were the Wheels. You needed the Handbooks, to "predict" what the Norwegians were going to do.

Yes, in the last moments of the Clinton era, I began to think that maybe it would not be All the Wheel anymore, but there'd be a new system or a new spirit of the law. It would start with ourselves, as lawyers. It would be a new sense of what the "law" is that we should give, or lay down, for ourselves. Be nice. Or be nicer. Do unto others, etc. Now, this may sound corny, and I mean this only in a relative way, but maybe we'd pick judges the way Scott would pick his jurors: Just pick them if they're nice people.

It might not change the inequality, but that might be okay if at the end of all our lawyering, we didn't feel like shit. Maybe we'd stop the war of all against all. Everything would settle, regardless, but now the settlements would be nicer. Why aren't they?

Yes, the law we lay down for ourselves, in our own lives, the kind of law Kant talked about . . . *that* legal system I began to feel would change. That's exactly what I was thinking. And then came *Bush v. Gore.*

43. THE MYSTERIOUS MEANING
OF *BUSH V. GORE*

I suppose in terms of the Wheel it means I go back to being scared. So much for being nice and for judges who say, "Oh! How I miss my clients!" Here's how many district court judges the new Bush may name (with numbers from past presidents compared):

George W. Bush (projected)	150–175
Clinton (two terms)	317
Bush Sr. (one term)	155
Reagan (two terms)	300

I can also stop trying, after Rolando, to change my life as a civil lawyer. *Bush v. Gore* has now taken care of that. For a few weeks after, the Big Question was: Why go back to being scared? I'm too old, give it up. Besides, it's not just the new judges, it's the way we got them. It's *Bush v. Gore* itself that scares me. It's hard to overstate that until the last minute even lawyers on the Left, like me, couldn't believe that Rehnquist, et al., would really *stop* the vote from being counted. Like children, we thought, No They Will Not Do It. And for days after, I'd sit at my desk and wait to see if a melancholy would take hold, to see if I could even pick up a Dictaphone, or hit voice mail, or if instead I'd say, "No, I've lost the faith." And not in an innocent way, like a whiskey priest who's still a believer, but in the way I might if the pope had come back from the dead, and said in Saint Peter's Square, "There's nothing, it's absolutely, absolutely ridiculous, and from now on, on the altars, all the Masses will be *black.*"

Since it's true I run to women first, for weeks I was going to write Sandra Day O'Connor. Just this:

Dear Justice O'Connor,
What you did was despicable.

And sign it, "A Member of the Bar." Maybe underline "despicable,"
so that she could hear the hiss. I asked friends, "Should I send it?"
"Sure." "Go ahead." One even phoned, "Did you send it?" I would
imagine that one night, alone in her office, she'd find and read my letter and know, for the first time, "I've . . . destroyed the Rule of Law,
haven't I?" Then she'd know what she'd done.

But later I wondered if she'd acted from a sense of honor. Maybe
she dreaded that if she'd let Gore win, the Right would try a coup.
Didn't I worry too? So she and Justice Kennedy may have felt, Better
to trample on the Rule of Law here, than have a coup, and end the
whole republic! And just as I was offering her little rice cakes in my
mind, I told my theory to my friend John, who laughed. "Yeah,"
he said. "You read how on election night all these people were with
O'Connor, and when at first they called Florida for Gore, she went
into a rage, and began knocking Gore, Gore was no good, and if Gore
was president, she could never step down?"

No, I hadn't read that.

So I went back to my other point, that if she had let Gore win, I
myself dreaded what would have happened. Thanks to *Bush v. Gore,* I
could duck the fight. O'Connor's vote had let me have it both ways.
I could fume and stamp my little feet, "Oh, they stole it!" But I didn't
have to hear them screaming.

Only by January did I realize that now as a civil lawyer I'd never get
the law I wanted. I could forget my post-Rolando projects. And as for
the Wheel? In two or three years, the Wheel would be a wheel of fire.
Just as I was feeling safe from it, too, safe from being burned with
sanctions. Even now after all the Clinton appointees, I know lawyers

who are scared to file. "But why?" I said to one. "There are only two or three bad ones."

"Only two or three?" he said. "Two or three is plenty!"

Now I shiver to think that in a year it will be five or six. The *Post* and *Times* say that in the White House now, a gaggle of Federalist types are screening the nominees. In a few months when I stand before my first W. Bush judge and look up, I may wonder, Was this the guy, in the back of Maggiano's, the one who said "Fuck you"?

Even in print it's risky for me to say that I wanted to practice a new kind of law. One day will someone cite those words to hang me? And yet though it's mad to write this, even as I hear the thunder booming, I still think that even after *Bush v. Gore,* or because of *Bush v. Gore,* we are still moving slowly toward a whole new sense of human rights. Sometimes I do think that we should be humble and just be a second chair at Twenty-sixth and Cal. And then I think, No, this is the time to be climbing to the golden courts above and arguing that in America, too, we should have human rights, more rights than we have ever dared to ask for before.

But that's mad. In the Bush era, how can it be that the human rights movement, a claim to more rights than before . . . how can all of that not be dead? It should be! And yet if it turns out, in two or three years from now, that my friends still find me in the practice of law, despite all the Bush appointees, I want to explain why I saw the beginnings of a new beginning.

Of course if I'm not practicing, they can skip this part.

*First Reason: We Finally Realized That Equal Protection
Was Not Enough Protection*

By this I mean, thanks to *Bush v. Gore,* lawyers on the Left and Center Left finally gave up pumping our Constitution and turned to human rights law. Long ago in law school I would not have believed we needed human rights, "U.N.-type" rights, right to a job, right to health, all those *words*. All we needed was our own human rights law, which was the Fourteenth Amendment, and Equal Protection. Yes I knew that once long ago in *Plessy v. Ferguson* the Supreme Court used Equal Protection to justify Jim Crow. But after Earl Warren took over Equal Protection and unstained it with his ablutions . . . after *Brown v. Board,* I was sure Equal Protection could not be so misused again.

Then came . . . *Bush v. Gore.* And once again Equal Protection is being used to keep blacks (at least in Florida) from voting. Now that I'm over fifty, I know, truly, at last, that the Constitution was not enough. In fact . . . isn't it like a Wheel? We stand there, before the Clerk of History, and we draw a . . . a Warren, then a Burger, then a Rehnquist, then another Rehnquist, then Rehnquist again! Why do we keep getting Rehnquist?

In law school I scoffed at human rights law, it isn't "real." But after *Bush v. Gore,* would I say the Constitution's real?

No, it's just the Wheel. In 1910, 1920, up to 1940, it's the Right's Wheel: They used it not just to uphold Jim Crow but to knock down labor laws, any good laws.

Then the Left, briefly, had the Wheel. Then, it was the Right's Wheel; nine times out of ten it's spinning right.

Okay, but now with these new judges to come, it would seem that human rights, as a different legal system . . . ah, I can kiss off that. Don't I know who's the president? Yes, I know. But in an odd way, Bush may be a good thing. Ever since he took office, the way he's been scrapping treaties . . . not just Kyoto, ABM, but even little ones about germs . . . it seems that unilaterally he's going to unify the Europeans. We may end up now with a hard-driving International Criminal Court. It's even an issue now for us Democrats, in a way that would be unthinkable if Gore had won.

So Bush may be a dawn of human rights law. Besides, there's the shock of *Bush v. Gore* itself. It was the moment that even some lawyers who just do mechanics' liens thought, Can this be the real law? Even *they* could see that the Constitution is the Wheel.

Already, of course, other lawyers, especially in criminal, are sneaking in human rights law. They already talk the talk. As a friend who does this work says, "Most people don't realize how much lawyers like us think this way now."

Instead of the *Harvard Law Review,* you read the latest report of Human Rights Watch. It's scary how it's now a way to "keep up," with what's happening in the law here, like having an advance sheet: yes, prison, death penalty, but even in labor law.

So with Bush in, I'm more interested in treaty law than ever. Even U.N. resolutions. In fact, my next trip to New York, I may even hop a cab and go look at the U.N. (Where is the thing, exactly?) Of late, I've even read the long reports of the Special Rapporteurs, who go on human rights missions. I read the long white papers, with forty or so recommendations on race relations, or prisons. Yes, I really find ideas I can use. I admit, though, for a lawyer, it's frustrating because there aren't a lot of "cases." But the treaties themselves are a kind of mind blow. In my middle age, when I'm stiff of brain, it can expand my sense of what the law can be.

I've just found the U.N. Convention for the Elimination of All Forms of Race Discrimination. It's not just a resolution or customary law, but *treaty* law, which we signed, as a party. It goes much farther than our Fourteenth Amendment, or civil rights law. It would prohibit a system of medical care like ours that would lead to any large racial disparity in terms of care—e.g., for blacks who have health insurance.

Imagine, we signed a treaty that makes our system of health care illegal. Or it would, except that we added a clause that if this treaty were to require America really to change anything, then it's null and void.

But the point is, human rights law now would change huge chunks of American law, especially criminal. It would change half the

shows we see on television. If you don't believe me, just scroll down
the U.N. Principles for Detention of Prisoners. Or the U.N. Convention Against Torture and Other Cruel, Inhuman, or Degrading Treat-
ment. When I was in law school, this was all a yawn. Now it's
fascinating. A lawyer friend says that the very existence of our brand-
new Super Max prisons, designed to inflict mental illness, are in flat
violation of U.N. treaty law.

But for me, the big shock is how it's changed my sense of what is
"okay" and "barbaric" in my specialty of labor law. Human Rights
Watch just put out a two-hundred-page report that lists every way
America is now violating international labor treaties. Some of it I
knew. The way companies can use scabs. Spy on workers. But treaty
law prohibits things I took for granted, such as "captive" meetings.
That's when Wal-Mart brings in Hispanic ladies and screams at them,
locked up there, for an hour, two hours, as to what evils will happen
to them if they vote in a union.

Of course it *is* barbaric. But I'd gotten used to it. Thanks in part
because I went to Twenty-sixth and Cal. I came indirectly to have a
new sense of labor law.

I should stop, but a lawyer friend, my age, tells a story about this.
Back in law school he went up to Jack Greenberg, famous civil rights
lawyer for the NAACP. "Oh, Mr. Greenberg," he said, "I want to be a
civil rights lawyer like you."

Greenberg only shook his head. "Ah," he said, "if I could do it
over, I'd go into human rights."

No kid then knew what he even meant. But now, in my own
case, if I ever did teach a course in law now, I'd start the kids off with
the last report of Human Rights Watch.

I finally realized the Constitution, American law, is not enough. That
the big problem is we don't have enough words. I once read that in

Weimar Germany, before Hitler, many liberals like me were "legal re-alists." Oh, it's all the Wheel, no matter what. Like Oliver Wendell Holmes, Jr., they'd say that the law was whatever the judges said it was. There was nothing up there, such as Natural Law, in the sky. But then came Hitler, and even some of the legal realists ended up in camps. And later, after the war, they said, "My God, it really can't be all the Wheel," since real judges had been up on Hitler's bench.

In short: Maybe there is something up there in the Sky.

Or at least they decided to put in more words, and rights . . . rights that would make us gasp. "My God, you can't put in a right to health care, or a right to a job."

Why not?

It's funny (I guess) how right-wing lawyers write best-selling books that tell us we're too rights-oriented and that if you compare our constitution to anyone else's, we have no rights at all. And where did "they" get these un-American rights?

Many come from the mother-of-all-human-rights documents, which is the U.N. Declaration of Human Rights, which was passed in 1948.

The Allies drafted it. The Europeans, in their constitutions, copied lots of it down. Now, if you scroll down the first few rights, they are the very basic ones, such as the right not to be tortured.

But keep scrolling, past number 10, then number 15, maybe start around 20, and you see: the right to health care, the right to be edu-cated, the right to a good job.

These are not individual rights, or civil rights, as we are used to thinking of them, but personal rights. Our rights to be persons, to de-velop our material and spiritual selves.

Indeed, the philosopher Jacques Maritain explains this all in a book. But after going on as I have about Montesquieu, I don't think anyone would tolerate a section here on Maritain.

The point is, we need to have these rights in writing. The Europeans, after the war, did it to prevent another Hitler. Maybe we didn't think we had to worry. But just in my own lifetime I have seen people at the bottom go from "poor" to "very poor" in a way even now many of us don't really grasp.

Because we didn't have the extra words, now, among other developed countries, we lead in inequality.

We really lead in poverty.

We lead even Burundi in our prison rate.

And we do Bangladesh-type things, such as putting kids in jail.

Our Constitution is not enough.

Second Reason: We Didn't Have to Win in Court

But how, with all these Bush judges, could we end up with a whole new legal system? Because we didn't win in court, in any 1960s sort of way. So how did we do it?

First, Mexico. It's on both sides of the border. That had to upend our legal system a little.

The historian Eric Hobsbawm points out that it's not just America but every European country, too, that is becoming a little like the Hapsburg Empire. Now, it's true that we've always been a nation of immigrants. But there's something different now. Mexico's new president, Vincente Fox, likes to say he is also the president of the Mexicans living here.

It's a long way from being the Dual Monarchy of Austro-Hungary, but it's also not quite like the old United States. It's like waking up and finding . . . not immigrants but another nation state in your bed.

So American law, very, very slowly, began to pick up the flavor of international law. Let me give an example.

Consider Article 36 of the Vienna Consular Convention. Years ago back in the Cold War, the U.S. actually signed this treaty, in part to protect our spies. The article says that if any foreign national is arrested, the police must inform such person that his or her consul can assist or help.

At the time (1965), our State Department didn't dream that one day about a third of Chicago would be Latino. So many an arrest now in Chicago triggers Article 36.

Now, in criminal law, no one has been released for an Article 36 violation. But the courts seem to say, Maybe in a civil case we will enforce this right.

And as more and more big cities start to comply, you have consulates monitoring the conduct of the cops. It's not just Al Sharpton, or even Jesse Jackson. It's Mexico, it's Germany. The whole world is coming now to Twenty-sixth and Cal.

Second, the WTO. I know it's not supposed to, but as I write this, it's become a place to file a lot of human rights briefs: e.g., how much AIDS drugs should cost in Africa, or whether the U.S. can impose sanctions on Cuba.

One day, just to get rid of all the briefs, they may set up a whole new global court.

Finally, the strange thing about human rights is that you can halfway win the case if you just stand up and *say it!* A friend of mine explained it, when I complained I couldn't find a case to support a human rights argument: "That's not how you do this law. You just *say* it's a human right! Don't you understand?"

Just say it.

After all, what can they really say on the other side? Because, let's face it, human rights can be a little vague.

The point is to make sure that it gets out to the public. And the more that a Robert Bork or Scalia scream about it, all the better. That's the best way we have to spread it through the culture.

In a way I even wonder, Do I even have to be a lawyer? The other night I was with a young, really young, married couple, and the guy, who had just quit a job at a bookstore, asked me about the law.

At first I thought he was asking should he go to law school? But I misheard.

"No, no, I want to help lawyers."

What?

"Helping lawyers . . . that's how I want to make a contribution." He wanted to do public relations for lawyers who were fighting for good causes.

PR . . . for lawyers?

"Because lawyers," he said, "they make us face up to things, that everyone else wants to turn away from."

At first I wanted to laugh. PR for lawyers? But the more he spoke, the more he persuaded me that since we don't try cases anymore or give speeches to juries, maybe we should consider hiring PR firms.

Especially in the case of human rights law, maybe PR is the way to do it. So at any rate, now when a young person asks me (and I should make clear, no one ever does), "Should I go to law school?," I might say, like Jack Greenberg, "Ah, if only I could do it all again, I'd go into PR."

Third Reason: Wasn't Human Rights Law Just Our Own Law Come Back to Us?

Because if I did go into PR, I'd know the spin I'd like to give to human rights law: "It's our own law come back to us."

If a new legal system is (as I believe) on its way to us, it will not have come about just because whites like me have become in America just another minority but because, as well, America itself was, is now, and always will be a house that could only have been built by human rights lawyers. The only reason we could think of to separate from Britain was to start to appeal to international law. The Declaration of Independence is just as far out as the U.N. Declaration of Human Rights.

I used to wonder why we lost our sense of being part of a global movement, i.e., for *international* human rights. Jefferson, his whole party, had that sense, and in the end they wiped out the opposition. What happened to it?

I never really understood why we lost that original international-human-rights sense of the country, until I came across *Specimen Days,* by Walt Whitman. In the middle of the book, Whitman puts part of his diary from the Civil War, when at the bedsides of young Union soldiers he watches them die. In one passage he begins to rant and damn every nation of the world—Prussia, and the France of Louis Napoleon, and Britain too—because every single one of them supported the Confederacy, opposed the North. And I tried to imagine what it was like back then to be a citizen of what was the only sovereign state that was a *democracy:* the only one in the world! And to know that every other country more or less wished us ill. If there was a law of the nations, it seemed to be on the side of slavery.

But then came World War II, the defeat of fascists. And now American-type human rights did become in a formal way the law of nations. Only then something happened, and as if we resented all these other countries for converting, we seemed to turn away from the idea that there was any law but ours.

It's so sad because where did the U.N. Declaration (1948) come but from a speech by Franklin Roosevelt, the "Four Freedoms" (1941), just before the war? That speech also now seems lost to us. And while it's on the Internet, along with the Vulgate Bible, etc., I bet it doesn't get a lot of hits.

Yet it should, because it sets forth the reasons why America fought the war, to ensure the Four Freedoms, which are:

1. Freedom of speech. Everywhere. Even in Iran.
2. Freedom of worship. America, yes, but Bosnia, China, Afghanistan, too.
3. Freedom from "want." The shocking one. If there was economic growth, everyone in the world had a right to a minimum.
4. Freedom from fear. Even in America. That's the freedom our country will have when there are all these freedoms everywhere.

And if you go to the FDR Memorial and read all he said about international human rights, it may seem to you he was trying to lock up in U.N. resolutions to come what he couldn't get legislatively from the U.S. Senate here at home. He was appealing to human rights, so in America, in every state, not only New York but even Georgia, we'd have human rights at home.

To read that first U.N. Declaration, it haunts me now. FDR was already dead, and his widow Eleanor, and the aging young New Dealers who fought for the Declaration, with the right to a job, to an education, etc., they must have known their time was running out. It's as if at the end they tried to take the dream of the New Deal, and put it up there, on high, as an International Law, and let it circle the world, until one day things change here and we can't take it back again.

Yes, I can hope. I do hope.

Personally, I'm ready for the Four Freedoms, especially freedom from *fear*. Once I thought, That's easy, all I have to do is stop being a lawyer. But even if I stopped, I now know of course there are other, bigger things to fear. After all, I saw Rolando's cell.

And give up being a lawyer? I hate to say this, but being a lawyer, having to look up the law, has brought a kind of order in my personal life. Yes, I know, I'm the type, a common type, who can "see" something in the golden light, etc., and I don't really need the law. Like so many in this country, I know what is good and evil already. But that's why I'm glad, that over and over I have had to go to the library and look up what the law really is, not what I think is right, but what the law thinks, from a distance, from far away. In the same way, as a country, we dislike international law. We don't want to see how as a country, we look from a distance, from an outside point of view. We already know, don't we, what is right and wrong?

This is a point I have lifted whole from a much better mind than mine, Thomas Nagel. Anyway, so for me, so for my country. We both need something, an external point of view, to see ourselves as others see us. Yes, even if we know, already, as we do, that we are God's holy people. Because one day, when all the nations of the world stream to God's holy mountain, we may find there is a little place set aside, to be, just for us, "America's court."

Anyway, when once every ten years someone asks, "If you had to do it over, would you go back to law school?," I like to be reflective and give a thoughtful answer, and say . . . : "NO! Absolutely not. Never. Never would I do that again. Never."

But then I'd be a fool, wouldn't I? I often hate being a lawyer, even more after *Bush v. Gore:* After all, now what's the point? But even so in my own case, self-absorbed as I am, sitting in my room alone and writing away like this, I know that if I weren't a lawyer I'd be even worse.

More authentic. More whole. A more integrated person. I'd be just myself and not, at times, somebody else.

Being a lawyer, thank God, is a way of curing that.

ACKNOWLEDGMENTS

Writing a book beats trying a case, but it's still a lot of work. So above all I'm grateful to André Schiffrin for publishing, editing, and shaping what I gave him into a book. Thanks to Sarah Fan for her editorial skill and line-by-line first aid. Linda Healey had great ideas, all of which I used. I owe Tom Frank at least a dinner in Paris for his last minute help.

Thanks to everyone at our law firm, Len, Jorge, Ann, Chris, Sarah. Because of them, I do enjoy going to work.

And to my pal Tony Judge. For whatever he said or did to make me sit down and write.